» Simple Guides
PROTESTANT
TRADITION

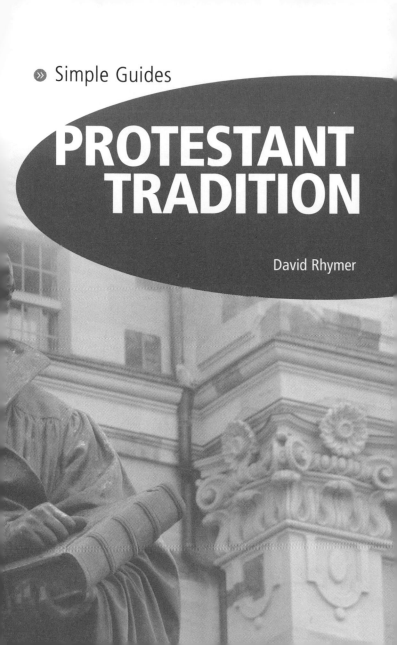

» Simple Guides

PROTESTANT TRADITION

David Rhymer

Published in Great Britain by
Simple Guides, an imprint of Bravo Ltd
59 Hutton Grove, London N12 8DS
www.kuperard.co.uk
Enquiries: office@kuperard.co.uk

First published 2001 by Global Books Ltd.
This edition published 2008

ISBN 978 1 85733 438 8

British Library Cataloguing in Publication Data
A CIP catalogue entry for this book
is available from the British Library

Printed in Malaysia

Cover image: Statue of Martin Luther outside the
Frauenkirche, Dresden. *istockphoto*
Drawings by Irene Sanderson

About the Author

DAVID RHYMER claims the distinction of being (probably!) the only confirmed Anglican, ordained Baptist, working Methodist minister in Britain. As such he has a wide experience of life in three of the main Protestant traditions, and has encountered a number of others through his ecumenical connections – which extend to a French Roman Catholic monastery. Having worked as a teacher, a Baptist minister and a Methodist minister, he is currently involved in adult theological education with Exeter University, and with adult training and education in the Methodist Church.

⊙ Contents

List of Illustrations

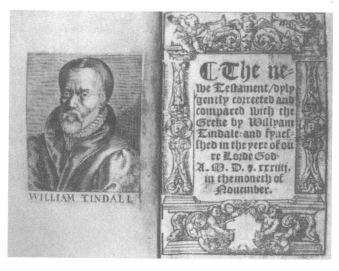

⊙ *The First Revision (1534) of William Tyndale's* New Testament in *English, showing title page with facing portrait. The First Edition was published in 1526*

There is a huge variety of interpretations of the word *Protestant* and this excellent introduction by David Rhymer makes this crystal clear. From the recent troubles in Ireland to the origins of the term in sixteenth-century Germany, this book describes for us the phenomenon and its development.

David Rhymer's text never loses clarity for the sake of brevity. He makes it clear, for example, that Anglicanism does not fall classically into the wider context of Protestantism but instead stands somewhere between Roman Catholicism and Protestant Christianity.

In describing the twentieth-century development of Protestantism we encounter a dazzling spectrum including Albert Schweitzer, Karl Barth, Dietrich Bonhoeffer and even Desmond Tutu.

This guide offers a map of the terrain which will be of use to a wide range of people. Those beginning to study the subject for the first time will be encouraged, and those who simply have a general interest will be stimulated and provoked – there could not be a better introduction.

STEPHEN PLATTEN
Dean of Norwich

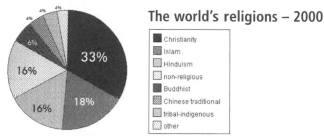

The world's religions – 2000

- Christianity
- Islam
- Hinduism
- non-religious
- Buddhist
- Chinese traditional
- tribal-indigenous
- other

⊙ *The world's population in the year 2000 was approximately 6 billion (6,000,000,000). Around 2 billion would consider themselves Christian, although this figure includes nominal adherents and also groups that may be regarded as being on the extreme fringes of mainstream Christian belief.*

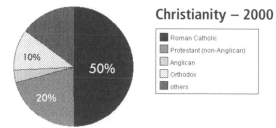

Christianity – 2000

- Roman Catholic
- Protestant (non-Anglican)
- Anglican
- Orthodox
- others

⊙ *Of the world's 2 billion Christians, 1 billion are Roman Catholic and 220 million are Orthodox. Just over 400 million are Protestant, of whom 200 million could be described as conservative/evangelical. 40 million of these are Baptists. There are around 70 million Anglicans world-wide. The remaining 300 million include some pentecostal groups who may not call themselves Protestant, but who may share some traditional Protestant beliefs. it is important to note that all churches and religious groups use different ways to calculate their membership.*

Why a book on 'the Protestant Tradition' at the start of the third millennium? Surely the Christian Church is trying to move on from the (all too often painful) divisions that have marked the story of the Church over the last thousand years? Well, yes, it is. It is to be hoped that the next thousand years will tell a very different story. But before the next chapter can be written we need to understand 'the story so far'. So this book is an attempt to do just that, and in so doing to introduce the reader to some of the significant people, events and ideas that have shaped a religious tradition that has influenced the history, culture and politics of the Western world for the last five hundred years, and which still influences the lives of around eight per cent of the world's population (a quarter of all Christians).

One thing you will soon discover is that 'Protestant' is a very wide-ranging term. A glance at a typical British town, for example, will reveal a variety of different 'Protestant' churches – Church of England, Methodist, Baptist, United Reformed, Brethren, Salvation Army, Pentecostal, Quaker, and probably one or two that you have never heard of before! And in North America you will come across around three hundred 'brands' of Protestantism – a number that continues to grow year by year. Yet within this diversity (and you only have to visit two or three different Protestant churches to discover just how diverse they are) there is a common (sometimes very thin!) thread of religious practice and belief that can be traced back to the people, ideas and events which rocked sixteenth-century Europe.

This book aims to help guide you through that diversity, as well as explore some of those religious practices and beliefs. For those who 'belong' within this tradition it should help them to understand where their particular bit of that tradition fits into the bigger picture. And for those who are simply curious it tells a story that certainly is not finished yet.

DAVID RHYMER

Chapter 1

Introduction: Some Essential History

Mention the word 'Protestant' and what springs to mind? For many in Britain, with Northern Ireland so much in the news over the last quarter of the twentieth century and the beginning of the twenty-first, the immediate thought is of strident voices raised in bitter, sectarian conflict, of political marches – even of terrorist murder. And what, many would go on to ask, has that to do with Christianity? Not a lot, you might think. But organized religion, as a product of human thought and a pattern for human behaviour, owes as much to external social, cultural and political influences as it does to profound beliefs concerning 'life, the universe and everything', And society, culture and politics have, in turn, been profoundly influenced by organized religion. This is as true of Christianity as it is of, say, Judaism or Islam – and is as true today as it has ever been.

The story of the Christian religion over the last two thousand years is proof of this: born out of revolutionary religious ferment in first-century Palestine; adopted by Constantine as the state religion of fourth-century Rome, and caught up with the declining years of the Roman Empire; preserving classical culture during the 'Dark Ages' and then fundamentally shaping medieval Europe,

ⓒ *Byzantine mosaic of St Paul, Ravenna*

giving divine authority to the claims of kings and emperors; inspiring the colonization of Africa, Asia and America; legitimizing wars and revolutions and influencing the science, art, philosophy and literature that is Western culture.

Of course, to speak of 'Christianity' as though it were a single coherent force and influence would be very far from the truth. The divisions, schisms and 'isms' of Christianity have had more influence on the shape of the history of the last two thousand years than any (mistaken!) notion of a single, united and harmonious 'community of faith'. And nowhere is this more true than in the case of the Protestant 'ism' of the last five centuries. The history of Christianity has been, amongst other things, a story of profound disagreements and of often acrimonious, sometimes violent, fragmentation. And this goes back to its earliest centuries.

Early Church History

As the towering might of Rome declined with the waning of the empire, various cities of the ancient Mediterranean world competed with each other for political influence. And religion was a major factor in this. The Church, and the bishop, of *Rome* claimed pre-eminence as the 'See of Saint Peter' and as the seat of the old empire, but other cities, notably Alexandria, Antioch, Jerusalem and, above all, Constantinople (where the seat of empire had moved in the fourth century) vied for power and influence.

Many of the early Christian debates about what was 'truth' and what was 'heresy' (out of which came the traditional 'creeds' of the Church) were often as much political as they were theological in origin. With the spread of Islam, some cities lost their influence over Christian affairs, others – Rome and Constantinople in particular – became dominant. They represented what was left of the 'Western' (Latin) and 'Eastern' (Greek) halves of the old empire. And in 1054 the two finally fell out with each other in an acrimonious division which still persists today, separating the 'Western' Church of Rome from the 'Eastern' Orthodox Churches – each claiming ancient apostolic authority for their beliefs and practices.

Our particular story continues with the 'Western' Church – the Church of Rome – which was, by then, inextricably caught up with the power, politics, society and culture of what we now call Western Europe. The Popes of Rome (with one or two notable 'hiccups') ruled as much as powerful princes as they did as pious prelates. Little could happen (they liked to think) in Western Christendom (as it was called) without their knowledge and approval. This, for example, was the time of the Crusades, which, while mainly directed at the Muslim occupiers of the Holy Land, also, on occasion, led to violent conflict with the Byzantine empire based in Constantinople.

A Time of Change

For nearly five hundred years the Church of Rome retained its powerful influence over Western Europe. But the world was changing. Constantinople fell in 1453, and the Muslim world was expanding, threatening the eastern flanks of European Christendom. Meanwhile, European explorers were reaching new shores in Africa, India, South-east Asia and China, and the Americas. On these fronts Europe was able to expand its political, cultural and, especially, religious influence.

Within Europe, new political concepts were also taking shape – princes and kings had aspirations to establish autonomous nation states. New alliances were being formed; new learning was questioning old ideas; new discoveries were changing people's lives – and, significantly, printing with movable type was prompting the growth of mass literacy. All of this meant that the way people thought was changing – and changing at an unprecedented pace. Clearly, this made for an explosive mixture. It was a German monk called Martin Luther who inadvertently lit the fuse.

Chapter 2

The 'Protest' in Protestantism

The Bible

One common aspect of all forms of Christianity is the Bible – consisting of the 'Old Testament' Hebrew scriptures (or 'holy writings') and the Christian 'New Testament'. (Christians may like to think that the 'Old' Testament belongs to them too, but they must not forget that it was, and still is, the book sacred to the Jewish religion.) Just as Judaism, as well as Islam, are 'religions of the book', so is Christianity. The reading and study of the Bible are important, to varying degrees, to all Christian Churches. It plays its part in public worship, in private devotion, in education and in the formation of Christian thought. But, like any other book, what you find in it depends on what you look for and, because it is quite a long book, most people (and therefore most Churches) tend to be selective about which bits they concentrate on.

The Orthodox Church, for example, is influenced especially by the writings of St John, traditionally regarded as the apostle who was closest to Jesus. Powerful images may be found in the metaphors and mysteries of the gospel, letters and 'Revelation' that bear his name. For example,

ⓒ *After a portrait of Martin Luther in an early account of his life and teachings*

the divine Logos ('Word'), 'the Light of the World' and 'the Lamb of God' are all significant images drawn from John, and they, amongst others, are central to the language, liturgy (formal patterns of prayer and worship) and art of Orthodoxy. This reflects, perhaps, this Church's close historic links with Asia Minor – the eastern end of the old Roman Empire – which has strong traditional connections with the apostle John.

The Church of Rome, on the other hand, had its own founding apostle – St Peter, traditionally regarded as the first 'bishop' of Rome. While his writings may not have amounted to much, his status as the original 'Rock' upon which Jesus was to build his Church and to whom the 'Keys of Heaven' were given (according to Matthew's gospel) gave him a unique authority, and gave Rome a unique position (as it claimed) of pre-eminence.

It is perhaps appropriate that a 'second generation' version of Christianity should find its inspiration from a 'second generation' apostle – St Paul (the one who saw the risen Jesus on the road to Damascus, some months after the first resurrection appearances to Peter, John and the other original apostles). Unlike the mystical poetry of St John, and the brief (and rarely read) epistles of St Peter, St Paul has left us with a significant chunk of our Christian scriptures through his powerful and carefully, and relentlessly, argued letters or epistles. St Paul offers us an incisive critique of both religion and society, with the clearly stated claim that Jesus Christ is Saviour and Lord of all the world, and further that faith in, and obedience to, Jesus is what constitutes God's purpose for humanity. In the light of this, all human beings, and all human systems and institutions (including 'religion') fall far short of the ideal. This argument, put forward most forcibly and systematically in his *Letter to the Church in Rome* (usually referred to as *Romans*), follows on from Paul's understanding of the gospel – the message of good news about Jesus to a world that desperately needed to hear it.

Martin Luther

It is little wonder, therefore, that this apostle, and this letter in particular (addressed, after all, to the 'Church in Rome') should provide the biblical authority for a theological protest against the *status quo* in the Church and in society. Which brings us neatly back to Martin Luther.

Martin Luther was an Augustinian monk as well as a university teacher. That he was a monk is significant because, as such, he was already part of a 'protest' movement. Despite the inevitable abuse and corruption of the intentions of their founders, the monastic orders of both the Roman and the Orthodox Churches (and the oldest orders pre-dated their division by several centuries) represented a desire for a simpler and more authentic way of being Christian.

The monastic movement first grew in the deserts of the Middle East and North Africa as a reaction against the growing complacency and compromise of the churches of the cities, with their wealth and privilege, as Christianity became comfortable and respectable in the late Roman world. (Interestingly, the monastic movement derived much of its theological impetus from St John.) Monasteries became places of great learning and scholarship, as well as of self-denying devotion, and over the centuries they attracted some of the most able thinkers and theologians of their day. And, as monks, they stood somewhat apart from the institutional Church, with its wealth and politics.

So in Martin Luther (1483–1546) we have a literate, scholarly man who, by all accounts, had a somewhat persistent and perfectionist personality. He was given to what we would call introspection and self-criticism. And it was this, first, that made him look for an answer to a nagging problem. Try as he might, he could not shake off a feeling of failure and guilt. He was a good monk; he did all that was required of him, and more. He performed all the required devotions, he prayed, he subjected himself to all the prescribed disciplines of his monastic order – he even went on pilgrimage to Rome. But nothing could lift his acute self-awareness of guilt and failure. The traditions of the Church could do nothing for him. The elaborate theology of Rome had no answer to the very personal question that Luther was asking.

But St Paul did! As Luther read Paul's *Letter to the Romans* he felt he was listening to a kindred spirit. He heard Paul agonizing (or so Luther thought) over the same issue of unresolved failure and guilt (have a look at *Romans* chapter 7 for the flavour). He thought that the shortcomings which Paul seemed to identify in the institutional Jewish religion of his day highlighted the same problems that he, Martin Luther, had encountered in the inability of the Church of Rome to meet his deepest needs. No amount of pious religious observance or agonized self-discipline could help Paul (or, rather, Saul of Tarsus as he was previously known) – any more than it could help Martin Luther. A religion based on pious 'good works' and strict obedience to ritual rules could not

⌄ *Luther preaching to his parishioners in Wittenberg, by Cranach the Elder*

address a deep personal awareness of guilt in the
eyes of God. Only God could do that, and his grace,
Luther learned from Paul, was totally unearned and
undeserved. It was the gift of Christ, not of the
Church, and to be received by faith.

Now, it has to be said that the earlier part of
this argument was probably not quite what Paul
meant. Paul, we should remember, had a very
high opinion of his own Jewish faith, and he
never rejected his fundamental Jewish beliefs.
He preached a profoundly Jewish message to
the pagan world of his day – but it was a Jewish
message with a huge difference, namely that it
declared that Jesus Christ is the Messiah and
Lord of the whole world, not just the Jews, thus
redefining the 'people of God' to include Gentiles
as well as Jews. This was the 'seismic shift'
prompted by Saul's remarkable experience on the
road to Damascus. But what I described earlier
was certainly how Martin Luther understood Paul
– medieval Catholicism was, for him, much the
same as first-century Judaism, and this idea has
stuck for five centuries in many Protestant circles.
So for Luther it was as though, as for Saul of
Tarsus, scales had fallen from his eyes. The
answer to his question was to be found in
scripture, not in the institutional Church, and that
answer was the grace of God through faith in
Jesus Christ.

Luther was not the first to query the theology
and practice of his Church, and to suggest instead
that the Bible itself held the answer to what we

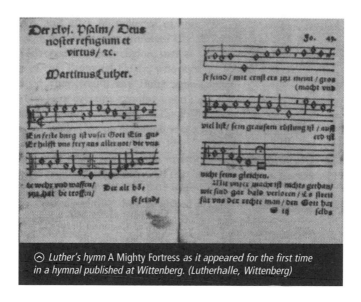

⊙ Luther's hymn A Mighty Fortress *as it appeared for the first time in a hymnal published at Wittenberg. (Lutherhalle, Wittenberg)*

would call 'the big questions of life'. Over the centuries, no doubt in part because of widespread illiteracy, the Church hierarchy had kept to itself the task of reading and interpreting the scriptures. It claimed that its authority and its practices were derived from its own traditions and earlier teaching, as well as from its interpretation of scripture. (All Churches do this, in fact – it was just that the Church of Rome was honest about it.) And so the interpretation of scripture was strictly the preserve of those who: a] had the authority of the Church to do it; b] did it in line with existing teaching; and c] could read (in Rome's case, Latin).

Protest

The move towards a more self-determined and 'Bible-based' religion can be traced back to people such as John Wyclif (1329–84) in England and John (Jan) Hus (1369–1415) in Bohemia. Both wanted to translate the Bible into the common spoken language (the vernacular) of the ordinary people. Ulrich von Hutten (1488–1523) and his friend Crotus Rubianus queried the value of the Church's elaborate rules and practices, as well as the power of the clergy to hold the people in fear while they themselves profited from the system (these, of course, are timeless protests!). A near

⊙ On a pole, in the form of a cross, hangs the papal authorization for the sale of indulgences. On the ground lie scales; two sacks of coins show the profit. (Woodcut by Jorg Breu the Elder)

contemporary of Luther, Desiderius Erasmus (1466–1536), a Dutch scholar, poured scorn on the complexities of the Church, urging instead a simple life based on a careful and informed reading of the Bible.

But Luther was the man for the moment. Yet he might have stayed in enlightened obscurity if it were not for politics and Church economics. One of the practices that had disillusioned Martin Luther was the profitable idea that the Church could offer time off from purgatory (the unpleasantly laxative-sounding period of purification between death and heaven – a non-Biblical but nonetheless powerful concept!) in return for a cash payment. This was called an indulgence – and a profitable business was to be had, not least if you owned some holy relics (fragments of the 'One True Cross', the bones or teeth of a saint, and so on) and could charge the faithful for the privilege of viewing them as the means to earning an indulgence.

Luther lived in Wittenberg, Germany, and the local prince, Frederick, had a lucrative relic collection. A particularly auspicious day for viewing relics was All Saints Day, 1 November. In 1517, the newly appointed Archbishop of Mainz, with large bills to pay and an eye to the Pope's favour (St Peter's basilica was being built in Rome, and a generous donation would not go amiss) sent his own 'relic road-show' to Wittenberg for All Saints Day. Frederick, fearing financial loss ('new' relics would divert the crowds from his) was more than happy to support Martin Luther's objections to this. Luther said that such exploitation of the religious fears of the people was quite wrong, that the Pope, if he had the control over purgatory that he claimed, should not use it for profit; and that, anyway, relics had little to offer compared to scripture. The last objection may not have thrilled Frederick, but it was too late to argue because, in time-honoured academic fashion, Luther added (for good measure) another ninety-two theological arguments (or 'theses') to the list and nailed all ninety-five to the church door!

Reformation

And that, in essence, is where the 'protest' in Protestantism comes from. (Strictly speaking, the term itself dates from 1529, when the German princes issued a 'Protest' against the political authority of the Pope.) One thing rapidly led to another, as much for political reasons as for theological, given the resentment, in Germany especially, of the Pope's interference in internal political and economic affairs. Despite banishment by the Emperor, and Rome's threat of excommunication, following the wonderfully named 1521 Diet of Worms ('diet' = imperial council, at a place called Worms), Luther stuck to his cause, aided by the recent invention of cheap mass printing which meant that his ideas spread around Europe in a very few years. His vernacular Bible followed quickly after, and became a classic of early German literature. And what was subsequently called the Reformation was under way.

Luther continued to follow his convictions, with a free conscience guided, he would have said, by the Holy Spirit. He began to query the traditional, and very powerful, role of the priesthood, questioning not only celibacy (non-marriage of clergy – Luther himself married in 1525) but also priestly authority, versus that of the Bible and of the conscience of the individual before God. In many respects Luther was a conservative, though – he retained some of the traditional views of the Mass, for example, arguing that while it was not a 'sacrifice' as such, the bread and wine were certainly changed into the body and blood of Christ. And he accepted the place of 'godly princes' in the order of things (perhaps because he had one or two friends in high places!). Others, however, seized the opportunity to go further. Some, more politically radical than Luther, sought social equality for the peasants. Others, more adventurous theologically, overturned many traditional readings of scripture, arguing for a more critical approach.

With the traditional status of the Pope, and of the Church of Rome, called into question; with the suggestion that God could be approached simply through faith in Christ, and not just via the authority of the Church; with the Bible in the vernacular (for those who could read, and for all who could hear); and with all claims to authority coming under scrutiny, an irreversible process of change was set in motion. Either the Christian faith was 'coming of age', or a potentially devastating 'Pandora's Box' had been opened. It all depended on how you looked at it.

Chapter 3

Early 'isms' & Schisms of Protestantism

A Divided Nation

A quick 'surf' of the 'World Wide Web' yields, in 2007, 18.3 million 'hits' for the word 'Protestant'. You can safely assume that thousands are constantly being added to that list. So this, be warned, is going to be a long chapter.

Protestantism, from its very beginning, has divided, amoeba-like (or, some would say, mutated) into more and more diverse variations on the original theme. This was inevitable, given its origins as a movement of protest. It has, ever since, had the negative tendency to define itself in terms of what it is not. It began as 'not the Church of Rome' and, very quickly, added 'and not like those Protestants over there, either!'. Protestants, indeed, are as likely to disagree with each other as they are to say 'we're not Roman Catholics'. From the earliest days of the Reformation, Protestantism has paid a high price for its emphasis on the freedom of the believer's conscience in matters of faith, with the result that its 'isms' have multiplied at an alarming rate.

*John Calvin as a young man.
His stern style of Reformation was
different from Luther's* ⊙

Lutheranism

Lutheranism flourished, as one might expect, in its home soil, as well as in Scandinavia. From Martin Luther himself came an emphasis on a deep personal piety, as well as an intellectual openness in the reading of scripture. His deep conservatism, however, was reflected in the preservation of many existing features of Church organization – he only differed from the Church of Rome if he believed it was required by a proper understanding of scripture. Eucharist (from a Greek word meaning 'thanksgiving') replaced the sacrificial notion of the Mass, but retained much of the outward form of the Roman service. Bishops still oversaw the priests (who could, at least, now marry).

The close links with the State which were there
at the beginning in Wittenberg were continued,
and Lutheranism became, in much of Germany
and Scandinavia, the State Church, with strong
economic and political ties between Church and
State. Through later nineteenth-century German
missionary activity (of which more later)
Lutheranism spread to America, via German
migrants, contributing yet another 'ism' to the
religious 'pick-and-mix' of the United States.

Calvinism

While Luther's concerns, perhaps, were more with
the individual's relationship with God (stemming
from his own experience), others sought to apply
'Biblical principles' to the ordering of society as a
whole. It is often the case that 'isms' that take their
names from their founders go far further than their
founders intended. That may well be the case with
Calvinism – or, there again, it may not.

John Calvin was, by all accounts, quite scary!
He was a brilliant lawyer and classical scholar, with
a ruthlessly analytical mind and awesome organiza-
tional ability. He lived in the Swiss city of Geneva.
The Reformation in Switzerland had developed
somewhat differently from that in Luther's
Germany. Huldrych Zwingli in Zurich followed a
rather less literal approach to the interpretation of
Biblical texts, especially with regard to the
Eucharist. He maintained that the bread and wine
only *represented*, rather than actually became, the

⊗ Lyons, France. A service in a converted private house called 'Paradise'. Anonymous painting of 1564. The sexes are segregated, and there is a clear distinction of rank in the seating. The preacher, hatted in the Calvinist manner, is timed by an hour-glass

body and blood of Jesus. Martin Bucer in Strasbourg moved further in the direction of lay Church government (power in the hands of the people, rather than the clergy).

In Geneva, John Calvin (1509–64) rose to prominence through the publication of his *Institutes of the Christian Religion* — a weighty handbook of Christian belief and practice. He advocated a rigorously systematic intellectual approach to Christian faith, alongside a deep personal piety (as with Luther) and his *Institutes* provided the framework for every aspect of daily life in Geneva, as well as for matters of faith, worship, preaching and Church discipline. Indeed, for Calvin, there was no real distinction between 'secular' (relating to human society) and 'spiritual' in the life of God's people.

Calvin's Geneva was ruled by strict principles, which governed work, family life, dress, recreation and all areas of public and private behaviour. Calvin also developed some key aspects of 'Reformed' teaching (to which we shall return later). Indeed, so influential has Calvin been, the term Reformed is usually used to refer specifically to Calvinist thought and practice. So, as his version of the Reformation spread to the Netherlands and Hungary, for example, the Reformed Churches founded there were entirely Calvinistic in nature. (The Dutch Reformed Church, so prominent in South Africa in the second half of the twentieth century, came via this route.)

The Calvinist form of Church government, by appointed Elders or Presbyters (from the Greek word for 'elder') gave rise to the alternative name of Presbyterian, which is the one that was used as the movement spread to England and Scotland, and from there to the east coast of North America, as well as Australia and New Zealand. The Dutch Reformed Church also spread out, to North America as well as to South Africa.

Anglicanism

As just mentioned, the Reformation spread to England in the form of Calvinist Prebyterianism. But here by far the most significant consequence of the upheavals in early sixteenth-century mainland Europe was, at first, political rather than theological. The story of the Church of England is a complex one that requires a chapter all to itself (Chapter 8), but its origins lay, not with monks or scholars, but with a King – Henry VIII. Henry wanted a son to succeed him to the throne. His first wife, Catherine of Aragon, had not produced one so Henry applied to the Pope for an 'annulment' (legal cancellation) of his marriage, arguing that Catherine was actually his sister-in-law (she was previously married to his late brother) so the marriage was not legally valid anyway. Unfortunately for Henry, Catherine was the Holy Roman Emperor's aunt, and the Pope was not inclined to upset such a powerful family. Henry, with some encouragement from those in Europe who opposed the Pope's influence, went ahead and married second wife Anne Boleyn despite Papal opposition.

⊙ *Henry VIII by Holbein the Younger (c. 1536)*

The following year, in 1534, Henry persuaded the English Parliament to pass the Act of Supremacy which declared that the King, and subsequent English monarchs, were 'the only Supreme Head on earth of the Church of England'. This gave Henry considerably greater marital freedom (he managed six wives in all, but no more than one, fortunately, at the same time) and also, conveniently, the opportunity to help himself to the vast wealth of the English Church and its prosperous abbeys (monastic establishments, with vast and profitable agricultural landholdings).

It would be wrong to infer that royal marital politics, and large amounts of land and money, were the sole factors in the English Reformation, so called (although even in early twenty-first century England they still play a part in public life). Henry may have had his own, rather obvious, agenda. But there were others whose minds were on higher things. William Tyndale (1494–1536) was determined to translate and publish a vernacular English Bible for the laity. He faced persecution, exile and, finally, burning at the stake.

Under Henry's son and successor, Edward VI, who came to the throne in 1547, the Archbishop of Canterbury (the leading Anglican churchman) was Thomas Cranmer (1489–1556). Cranmer attempted to carry through the Calvinist agenda. He emptied the churches of religious pictures, candles and priestly robes – the obvious visible marks of the Church of Rome. He accepted Zwingli's simplified view of the Eucharist, and generally tried to remove anything that seemed to have any connection with Rome. In 1549 he published the *Book of Common Prayer*, a model of reformed Anglican belief and practice. This was perhaps the closest that England ever came to having a thorough-going Protestant State Church (apart from the later brief revolutionary period under Cromwell, to which we shall return), but it was not to last.

Edward's reign was short-lived, and on his death in 1553 one of Henry's two daughters, Mary Tudor, came to the throne, despite Cranmer's best efforts to thwart her. Mary had remained a staunch follower of the Church of Rome, and Cranmer saw this as the likely end of the reformation of English church life. He therefore supported Lady Jane Grey as Edward's successor – a rash move that led to him being accused of treason. He escaped the (usually inevitable, and always fatal) consequences of that charge, only then to be accused of heresy, which would usually result in a very similar fate, the only difference being that the end would come by burning at the stake rather than beheading on the block.

At this point poor Cranmer's courage failed him (one may sympathize) and he publicly 'recanted' (withdrew) his Protestant beliefs and his rejection of the supremacy of the Pope, but they burned him anyway, in the charitable belief that it would be good for his soul. Cranmer retrieved his dignity at the last minute, and plunged the offending hand that had signed his recantation into the flames as they rose around him.

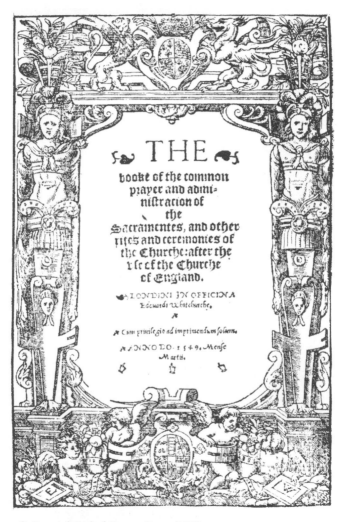

Cranmer's Book of Common Prayer *(1549)*

⊙ *Thomas Cranmer holding the Epistles of St Paul, by Gerhardt Flicke*

The fate of Thomas Cranmer illustrates a sad feature of Christianity (not unique, though, to this particular religion). When it comes to disputes about religious belief the conviction that 'we're right, you're wrong!' can be the excuse for behaving in ways that seem to contradict fundamental notions like 'love your enemy'. Perhaps the real problems arise with loving those who are meant to be on the same side. Of course, Cranmer lived (and died) in an age where political violence was commonplace. But religious conviction fuelled that violence and the conflicts between 'Catholic' and 'Protestant' have been some of the most bloody of the last five hundred years. The problems of Northern Ireland, for example, are the result of the enforced suppression of Irish Catholics by the creation, under James I, of a settlement of Scottish and English Protestants in Ulster.

Under Mary Protestants were treated even worse than Catholics had been under Henry, and England grew tired of religious bloodshed as 'Roman' practices were forcibly reintroduced. Her sister, Elizabeth I (1533–1603), came to the throne five years later (in 1558) and she, with the consummate political skill of her father, established a settlement – the peculiarly Anglican *via media* ('middle way'). The break with Rome, and the undermining of the power and wealth of the Church, had been welcomed by some in England – in part, at least, because of the innate English suspicion of anything that looked or sounded 'foreign'. And the move towards a more austere, 'rational' and 'bookish' kind of Christianity had an appeal to scholarly Englishmen. But for many others the break with Rome, with its colourful and familiar practices, was a considerable wrench. And many, too, had significant intellectual and theological objections to Protestantism. Indeed, it has been suggested that the majority of the English felt a deep affinity with their 'old' religion.

A modified form of Protestantism, which did not involve too much social upheaval and which retained many features of traditional Catholicism, was more likely to receive popular support. And that is what Elizabeth, wisely, sought to achieve. Politically, a balance was achieved in Parliament with a nominally Protestant (and therefore loyal to the Crown) House of Commons. Roman Catholics could not become Members of Parliament for another two-and-a-half centuries. The nonelected upper chamber – the House of Lords – still reflected the interests of the 'old' land-owning and wealthy conservative Catholic aristocracy, who were anxious to keep the bleak Swiss excesses of the European Reformation at arm's length.

Thus, a peculiarly English version of Protestantism was imposed: Anglicanism. Nothing theologically extreme – no Calvinism here. Rather, it was a toned-down version of the familiar practice of the Church of Rome, with the Pope and Latin replaced by the monarch and English, but still with bishops and priests (who no longer had to be celibate). Holy Communion replaced the

Mass, with Protestant features mingled with Roman tradition, including some aspects previously removed by Edward. Church buildings were retained, with monastic abbeys becoming cathedrals and carrying on much as before, but without the monks. In some respects Anglicanism resembled the Lutheran form of Protestantism, and indeed by the close of the twentieth century the two traditions had begun to explore their common ground in fruitful ecumenical dialogue, with the promise of the process continuing for some time to come.

One curious feature of the history of the United Kingdom is that the Anglican Church of *England* is the Established Church in England only. In Scotland the Established Church (the Church of Scotland) is distinctly Presbyterian, although the monarch is still its official head. Wales and Ireland add further complications, the history of the latter bringing us the wonderful word 'antidisestablishmentarianism'. Beyond the British Isles Anglicanism has travelled widely – to America, where it is called the Episcopalian Church ('episcopal' = governed by bishops); and via the British Empire (along with other curious features of 'Englishness') to Australia, New Zealand, South Africa and Canada, and to its colonies in Africa, the Caribbean, India, Hong Kong and Polynesia.

Today, the many Churches of the 'Anglican Communion' represent a very diverse mix – as does the Church of England itself, to which we must return in Chapter 8.

So far, we have looked at three early strands that arose out of the reforming movements of the first half of the sixteenth century. These are the ones that have been most caught up with politics and national identity.

But Protestantism did not stop there. The Protestant family tree rapidly grew into a forest, with the result that it can be hard to see how the branches fit together.

The Radical Reformers

For some, the mainstream Reformation was simply not radical enough. Too much existing 'Roman' practice was retained and the traditional ordering of 'bishops, priests and deacons' went unchallenged. German or English may have replaced Latin as the language of preaching and worship, but the content was, in many respects, little changed. However, the Bible, especially the parts of the New Testament that reflected the life and practice of the first-century Church, offered another, altogether more exciting, prospect.

For example, even a superficial reading of the four gospels, the Acts of the Apostles and the letters of St Paul reveals that *infant* baptism was never explicitly mentioned. Rather, the baptism of 'confessing believers' was the common practice for the 'early Church'. Observations like this quickly led some to question whether the principal reformers were going far enough or fast enough with the agenda for change in accord with the teaching of scripture. Infant baptism was firmly part of Christian tradition and it was inextricably tied to all kinds of fundamental issues concerning faith and 'belonging', the doctrine of sinful human nature and the status of the Church, as well as questions of power and control. Admission to the Church, and thus to citizenship and, finally, heaven, was via baptism. And the Church, be it Roman or Reformed, kept firm control of that. To question the legitimacy of infant baptism was thus to raise all kinds of questions about the nature of Church and society because, in a Lutheran, Calvinist or Anglican State, everyone was baptized into the Church as a matter of course.

So it was scandalous, to say the least, when a group of 'radicals' began to baptize as 'believers' adults who had previously been baptized as infants. This may have been a logical development of Luther's insistence on 'faith alone', but it caused a stir in Zurich in 1525, and led to (sometimes violent –'Drowning's too good for them!') persecution of the Anabaptists or 're-baptizers'. For the Anabaptists, the community of faith was necessarily one of absolute equality, and no distinction was made between a 'lay person' and an ordained minister – another threat to the orderly structure of society.

Such 'enthusiasm' led to tragic results in the German town of Munster in the early 1530s, where a group of Anabaptists declared that the Kingdom of God was nigh, and about to be established, by force if necessary. Such dangerous ideas could not be tolerated, and both Catholic and Protestant civil authorities were united in supporting a bloody suppression of the town. After that cautionary experience, Anabaptists turned more towards Pietism, Separatism and Quietism (words which mean just what they suggest: a pious, separate and quiet way of life).

One such group, in Holland, under the leadership of Menno Simons (1496–1561), a former Dutch priest, followed this course. The Mennonites were largely tolerated as an odd, but harmless, sect. Some Mennonites withdrew to more isolated rural areas – notably as early settlers in North America. One well-known vestige of that migration is found in the Amish farming communities of Pennsylvania and Ontario. Closer to the mainstream of the European Reformation there were others, such as the Puritans, who were influenced by Anabaptist thinking but who did not withdraw from society in the same way. We return to them a little later.

Once cherished Church traditions, even ancient ones, are held up for comparison with the practice of the New Testament churches, other conclusions may follow. The Creeds of the Church are a product of the early centuries of Christian theological debate, and they state doctrines, or teachings, that are not necessarily found in the New Testament but which may (sometimes with a considerable amount of imagination) be derived from it. 'Not good enough!', some said. The doctrine of 'God in three persons' – the Trinity – is not explicitly stated in the New Testament. Neither is there any clear and unequivocal assertion of the divinity of Jesus Christ (nowhere does it say precisely, 'Jesus is the eternally divine Son of God').

Both doctrines may be said to follow fairly obviously from New Testament tradition (although the Trinity is a notoriously difficult concept to grasp), but they were not necessarily part of the belief system of the very first Christians. Thus, some in the sixteenth century went as far as to deny these two central doctrines – again, to the horror of both Catholic and Protestant authorities, with inevitable consequences. Unitarian ideas, as they are described, have cropped up from time to time in subsequent centuries, but have only been tolerated in the last two hundred years, often as 'liberal' offshoots of other, more conservative groups (as in the case of Baptists – see below).

Some who were caught up in the more extreme radical aspects of the Reformation opted for separation, even self-imposed exile, in order to follow their consciences. These are often known as Separatists. Some, over time, formed break-away sects that then developed their own tradition and spawned further offshoots – an all too frequent feature of Protestantism. But others still tried to remain in the mainstream, raising a radical voice from within. This was the case with those who came to be called Puritans, who campaigned for a more pure form of religion. There were such voices within Elizabeth's Church of England – passionate Protestants who had been exiled during Mary's bloody reign, and who had absorbed Calvinist teaching in Geneva and elsewhere. On their return they were determined to make the Church of England a thoroughgoing Protestant movement, with no vestiges of former 'Romish' customs and practices. They in turn were opposed by vigorous anti-Calvinists within the Church. That the Church of England could ultimately embrace both extremes at once is a mark, perhaps, of Elizabeth's success – or an indication of hopeless theological woolliness. Opinions vary!

The Puritans gave rise to the term 'puritanical' – a good indication of where they stood on moral matters. They were sober in every sense of the word: frugal and hard-working and tireless in urging moral rectitude. Their influence did not last for more than a century within the Church of England but, while it did, it was significant. John Milton's poetry and John Bunyan's *Pilgrim's Progress* give us windows into Puritan thought. The notion of the Protestant work ethic stems from the Puritan emphasis on hard work and modest living. While it may have faded in later seventeenth-century England,

Puritanism had, by then, a firm hold in parts of North America.

Martin Luther would have been amazed at what happened within just one life-time of his nailing his ninety-five earnest and, to us, often obscure arguments to a church door. (Somehow it is hard to imagine a 'Post-It' note having a similar effect!) But it transformed the face of Europe and ultimately, much of the world (not least, as we may have guessed already, by its formative influence on North America). And it gave us the Protestant Tradition.

Chapter 4

The Next 100 Years & Some More 'isms'

All this history may seem a long time ago (history is often like that) but I hope you can see why it is important if we are going to understand this phenomenon we call Protestantism – not least the exponential proliferation of Protestant websites. And we have not finished yet – the seventeenth century saw the emergence of yet more variations on the Protestant theme, some of which you could probably see coming several decades before.

We have already noted how differing views of the best way to govern the Church began to emerge, once the traditional order of bishops, priests and deacons was called into question. So, for example, if there was no real difference at all between 'lay' and 'ordained' people, one could then speak of the priesthood of all believers (an idea with some good New Testament precedents). And then one might conclude that the people of God gathered together for prayer, worship and teaching (the congregation) were able, under the guidance of the Holy Spirit, to determine God's will for their shared life and practice. And that is precisely the idea that emerged, initially amongst the followers of Martin Bucer in Strasbourg and, more radically, amongst the Anabaptists.

Family of sixteenth-century Hutterites (a Lutheran sect), from the title page of a book defending the Anabaptists (1589)

This kind of thinking travelled back to England after the period of European exile endured by many during the reign of Mary. Separatist clergy began to see the local congregation, rather than a national (and worldly) institution, as the authentic manifestation of the Church of Jesus Christ. And here we find the beginnings of what became Congregational churches, as well as a contributory factor in the thinking of the early Baptists.

Congregationalism is characterized by its approach to Church government; in its beliefs more generally it was essentially the same as Presbyterian Calvinism. (In England the United Reformed Church is a fairly recent [1972] amalgamation of the Congregational Union of 1832 and the English Presbyterian Church. Some Congregational churches also entered local 'Unions' with Baptist churches in the earlier part of the twentieth century.)

In North America (as ever, fertile ground for 'isms') Congregationalism was embraced by early Puritan settlers. (Harvard and Yale Universities were both founded by Congregationalists for the education of their ministers.) Perhaps the most famous of these American Puritans were the Pilgrim Fathers who sailed on *The Mayflower* from Plymouth, England, in 1620, and founded Plymouth Colony in south-east Massachusetts.

Baptists

The Baptists (and I count myself among their number) have somewhat uncertain origins. Experts cannot agree as to whether their roots lie in European Anabaptism, or in English Separatism. The answer, probably, is not either/or, but both. Elizabeth's Anglican compromise was not congenial to some Separatists, who preferred voluntary exile in Europe to conformity to the Church of England. These were the early Dissenters whose religious consciences would not allow them to belong to the national Church. Some of these Separatists almost certainly

⊙ *A nineteenth-century picture of the first Thanksgiving Day, November 1621, when the Puritans thanked God for their first year in America*

came into contact with Anabaptists in the early part of the seventeenth century – probably in Amsterdam.

The result was that, in 1612, a Separatist Congregational church practising 'believer's baptism' was established in London by a group of returned exiles under the leadership of Thomas Helwys. This is generally regarded as the first English Baptist church. The earliest 'General' Baptists were not Calvinistic in doctrine, believing rather that salvation was available to people in general, not just a particular few (we will discuss the wonders of Protestant beliefs in due course).

The Calvinist 'Particular' Baptists (sometimes known as 'Strict and Particular') appeared in the

1630s. The subsequent relationship between the two branches has not always been a happy one, leading, notably, to the dramatic departure (in 1887) of the Calvinist Charles Spurgeon, the Victorian 'Prince of Preachers', from what he saw as the doctrinally 'wishy-washy' Baptist Union.

Baptists have had their own significant impact on Protestantism. They founded the oldest surviving training academy for dissenting ministers (now Bristol Baptist College) in 1679 and have produced many notable scholars. The Baptist Missionary Society, founded in 1 792 by William Carey, was the first 'modern' overseas missionary movement. And they gave the world Martin Luther King and Billy Graham, arguably two of the best known Christian leaders of the twentieth century. In America the Baptists have become the largest Protestant denomination – the result, initially, of the Great Awakening, a massive religious revival of the mid-eighteenth century, and subsequently by their powerful appeal to Black Americans. Baptist churches (Baptists use the word 'church' only for their local congregations, not for national or denominational bodies) represent a distinctive feature of Protestantism – Evangelicalism (which, along with Fundamentalism, we discuss later).

With the 1662 Act of Uniformity, which imposed compulsory membership of the Church of England, the 'Dissent' of the early seventeenth century became known as Nonconformity. It is therefore historically inaccurate to use terms such as

'Nonconformist' or 'dissenting' to describe later developments, notably the Methodism of the eighteenth century, or the Pentecostalism of the early twentieth. The more general term Free Churches is often used to include all those Protestant Churches which are not 'established'. But the older terms can be used for one of the more significant, if not large, religious movements of the seventeenth century – the Quakers.

Quakers and Shakers

It is interesting that, while the Reformation proper happened first in mainland Europe, it is England that gave rise to many, if not most, of the Protestant movements that have achieved worldwide prominence. The Quakers (known from the nineteenth century as the Religious Society of Friends) began with George Fox (1624–91). Fox believed he had discovered that the 'inner light' of Christ could be experienced without any reliance on the practices, sacraments and teaching of organized religion. This was, perhaps, the logical conclusion of following one's own conscience under the guidance of the Holy Spirit. It was Christianity without any of the trappings of 'religion'.

Fox was a transparently sincere and good man, and he drew a group around him who were known first as 'Friends of the Truth' – later nicknamed 'Quakers' because Fox urged people to 'tremble before the Lord'. Unfortunately, although they were entirely innocuous and inoffensive people, Quakers suffered cruel persecution from their Protestant neighbours, forcing some to escape to the religious freedom of the young colony of America.

Pennsylvania was founded by William Penn in 1682 to offer Quakers a safe haven. Quakers have always been determined pacifists – and as staunch conscientious objectors they founded the 'Friends' Ambulance Corps' to provide wartime relief to the injured of all sides. Their meetings, in starkly simple meeting houses and in profound silence, only broken by occasional spontaneous spiritual reflections, still draw those who are looking for something unavailable in other, less tranquil, forms of worship.

One notable offshoot from the Quakers were the similarly named Shakers, who, under Mother Ann Lee (c1738-84) emigrated to New York in 1774. There are only a handful of Shakers left today, but their distinctive hand-made furniture has survived their eccentric style of worship, which involved a form of religious line-dancing, marching, laughing, barking, extremely loud singing and their trademark violent trembling. (Shaker chairs were designed to be hung on the wall to make room for their rather energetic services.)

Having noted the wide variety of Protestant practices, it will come as no surprise to discover that Protestant beliefs are equally diverse.

The Orthodox true Minifter,   the Seducer and falfe Prophet.

⊙ A sixteenth-century pro-Anglican woodcut contrasts the 'Orthodox true
Minister' preaching in church, with the Separatist 'Seducer and false Prophet'
preaching from a tavern window

Chapter 5

What Protestants Believe

The Creeds

Any statement that begins, 'Protestants believe . . .' is almost bound to be wrong. This must be quite apparent by now, not least from what we have seen in the last two chapters. 'Protestant' is such a broad category that it defies easy definition, either in historical or theological terms. But do they have more in common than 'not Roman Catholic or Orthodox'? We can, perhaps, identify some broad trends – always bearing in mind that someone, somewhere, will probably believe something quite different.

Allowing for the protests of Unitarians (and some Quakers), we can safely say that almost all Protestants believe in God as commonly understood by Christians – Father, Son and Holy Spirit. Some may question the external, objective reality of God as a supernatural being (seeing 'God', perhaps, as a way of talking about our highest human aspirations), but even so the language of 'God' is something that Protestants share with all other Christians.

Can we go further and say that Protestants accept the traditional historic Creeds of the early

⊙ *Bible title page, published 1535*

centuries of the Church – those ancient statements
that begin, 'We believe in God . . .'? Well, yes and
no! Allowing (inevitably) for all the various
possibilities of interpreting what the Creeds really
mean (and it is hard enough to work out what that
meant when they were first composed) there are
probably various aspects of the formal Creeds that
many Protestants would want to query or re-write.
But most Protestants (like most Roman Catholics
and Orthodox believers) will happily recite one of
the traditional Creeds within an act of worship as a

broad consensus statement of Christian belief.

But not all. Some branches of Protestantism (and, as suggested earlier, it is not always obvious that we are all in the same tree!) refuse to subscribe to credal statements as a matter of fundamental principle. That is certainly true of Quakers and most Baptists, for example, and much of the evangelical tradition within Protestantism. They would want to say, and say with a passion and conviction that can be quite daunting at times, 'We believe in God as *revealed in Scripture*'.

The Bible

And this, of course, takes us right back to one of the fundamental aspects of the Reformation – the assertion, by Martin Luther, that the Bible contains all the truth necessary for a 'saving knowledge of God'. (Although Luther, and Calvin, also accepted the historic Creeds as part of the essential tradition of the universal Church.) So do *all Protestants* 'believe the Bible'? Well, yes and no! Sorry, but it is really not as simple as the title of this book might suggest. First of all, there has been disagreement even about the contents of the Bible, let alone its authority and its meaning. Martin Luther himself had grave doubts about the New Testament letter of James ('an epistle of straw'), as well as the letters of Peter and the Book of Revelation. What we call the canon, or authoritative benchmark of scripture – its officially recognized 'contents page' – was not always agreed, even in the sixteenth century. The so-called 'Protestant canon' that we have today is significantly shorter than the Roman Catholic one, which includes a 'second canon' of additional bits – rather disparagingly called the Apocrypha by Protestants.

The issue is further complicated by the problem of translation. A notable feature of the Reformation was the translation and printing of the Bible in the vernacular language of sixteenth-century readers. Previously the Latin Vulgate had been the only accepted translation of the Church of Rome. This translation was regarded as authoritative and accurate in all respects. Now, translation is not a precise science – unlike deciphering a message written in code. Words in one language can have several possible meanings in another, and grammar varies widely as well, so any translation is only an approximate version of what was written in the original. Look at the English translation of the instructions for assembling a 'do-it-yourself' cabinet made in Korea and you will get the general idea. And when the text in question is supposed to be revealing the truth about *God*, the problem is much more acute.

The result of all this is that any translation of the Bible is determined by decisions made by the translators, and so no two translations will come out exactly the same. This is not a problem if you have only one 'authorized' version, but it can be a problem when translations multiply, as they did rapidly following the Reformation. Churches may have attempted to retain control of this – hence

⊙ The interior of an eighteenth-century Dissenters' meeting house. The atmosphere is that of the debating hall – far removed from the devotion and mystery of the medieval cathedral

the Authorised King James Version, for example –
but the price paid for this is a suppression of
honest scholarship and freedom of thought.
And both of these are (or should be) cherished
concepts for Protestants.

This discussion is not a diversion from the
question asked a page or two ago. If we are going
to say, 'Protestants believe the Bible' we have to
ask 'whose Bible?'. That is one inevitable
consequence of the Reformation. Another inevitable
consequence is that once *interpretation* of the Bible
was set free from the tradition and authority of the
Church, a whole host of possible meanings began
to emerge. The Magisterium, or 'Teaching Office' of
the Church of Rome gave the Church the definitive
and non-negotiable meaning of the scriptures. And
there is a lot to be said for that! It saves a great
deal of argument which, inevitably, has been a
major characteristic of the Protestant tradition. We
saw it in the earliest stages over something as
apparently simple as 'Take, eat, this is my body . . .'.
Luther, Calvin and Zwingli could not agree on what
Jesus meant by those few words, and Protestants
have cheerfully carried on this and numerous other
debates ever since.

What this does reveal, though, is that reading,
and especially preaching, the Bible is, and always
has been, a central feature of much of the
Protestant tradition, as is personal devotional Bible
reading. We may not agree on what it means, but
we know the debate is an important one, because
the Bible does play a central part in almost all

variants of Protestantism, and its critical and
scholarly study has been one major consequence of
the Reformation – both in the Protestant tradition
and, increasingly through the twentieth century, in
the Roman Catholic Church too.

Protestants, in general, would claim that the
Bible is the 'primary source' for knowledge about
God and for guidance on 'Christian living'. They
would also claim that their own particular traditions
and practices have some kind of biblical foundation
and authority. The fact that they can draw so many
different, even contradictory, conclusions is, as we
have observed, the price to be paid for allowing
people to make up their own minds. (The distinctive
view of the Bible held by Fundamentalists will be
examined later.)

Faith

The Protestant tradition has tended, following
Martin Luther, to place some considerable
emphasis on the importance of personal faith: *solo
fides* – 'faith alone'. This means both the content of
faith, expressed as 'We believe in . . .' and also the
act of faith – the decision of personal commitment.
Luther derived this from St Paul in particular,
notably from passages such as Romans 10:9 - '. . . *if
you confess with your lips that Jesus is Lord and
believe in your heart that God raised him from the
dead, you will be saved'*.

Most (but by no means all) variants of
Protestantism regard membership of the Church as

conditional upon some kind of declaration of faith, of both the 'I believe . . .' and 'I have decided to . . .' varieties, although the emphasis varies. Some traditions (such as the more Calvinistic Reformed Churches) require assent to a formal Creed or 'Confession' (such as the 1647 Westminster Confession of Faith), others (such as the Church of England) have used a form of 'Catechism', or formal question-and-answer declaration of faith. Others again may require only the most basic 'I believe . . .' statement, supported by a personal statement of commitment, or 'testimony'. This would be common in the more evangelical Protestant offshoots (such as Baptist churches).

For Martin Luther, personal faith was not some kind of optional extra for church enthusiasts. Rather it was essential to personal salvation (acceptance by God). Justification by faith, as it is called, has been one of the great rallying cries of traditional Protestantism.

Baptism and Confirmation

Given this stress on personal faith, in terms of both belief and commitment, it is not surprising to find that infant baptism, where practised, tends to be a somewhat low-key affair – the real business being reserved for some later adult rite of passage, such as confirmation. Baptism itself is a ritual washing with water to symbolize God's forgiveness and acceptance. So, in the Church of England, for example, baptism (or christening) usually takes place in the parish church, often as a modest private ceremony, conducted by the local vicar, while confirmation is a grand occasion presided over by the bishop himself, often in the full splendour of a cathedral service. Baptist churches (and others who do not practise infant baptism) avoid this oddity by only baptizing believers 'upon profession of faith', making this a very significant and, where done by total immersion, very wet rite of passage.

It has to be said (regardless of any Baptist prejudice!) that there is an unresolved tension in the common Protestant practice of baptizing infants, but reserving full admission to the Church for those who make a later declaration of faith.

⊘ *Believer's baptism by total immersion in a modern Baptist church (showing author in action!)*

This is well illustrated by the fact that in many Churches it is not simply the *baptized* who take Communion, but only the *confirmed*. So to a visitor to a church (and this is as true of Roman Catholic and Orthodox Churches as of Protestant) it may be by no means clear whether or not they are welcome to receive Communion (not least because some Churches may not recognize baptisms in another Church as valid – a further, and very unhappy, complication).

Communion

It has to be said that there is a bewildering array of beliefs in this area. The early debates between Luther and Zwingli have never been resolved, as becomes obvious when you consider the variety of names given to the central rite of the Christian Church, modelled on Jesus' 'Last Supper' with his disciples on the night before he was crucified. For some it is still 'Mass' (notably at midnight on Christmas Eve). For others it is 'Eucharist' (from the Greek word for 'thanksgiving') or 'Holy Communion'. Or it may be 'The Breaking of Bread' or 'The Lord's Supper'.

Each name reveals something of the belief that lies behind it. This may be the more evangelical understanding that the sharing of bread and wine is simply an act of fellowship or 'communion' with the risen Christ, present through his 'body' (the gathered community of believers). Or it might be a 'memorial' of his death (as with Zwingli) – again, a view held by some evangelicals.

Others hold a more 'sacramental' concept of something significant occurring as certain words are said and certain actions performed (Luther's view). Anglicans (being a peculiar Catholic/Protestant hybrid) may hold any view, including the full-blown traditional Roman Catholic belief that the bread and wine change in some mysterious way into the actual body and blood of Christ, so that his sacrifice is re-enacted on the altar. We shall return to the various ways in which Communion is actually celebrated when we look in more detail at worship in the Protestant tradition.

Sacraments

The preceding comments on baptism and Communion introduce another important Protestant variation from the traditional teaching of the Church of Rome. Luther, you may recall, was very concerned about the abuse of 'relics' – holy *objets d'art* or fragments of deceased saints' bodies, or whatever – and the idea that the Church could somehow dispense God's grace in return for a financial consideration. This is linked to the idea of sacraments, traditionally defined (as in the Anglican Prayer Book) as 'outward and visible signs of an inward and spiritual grace'. The Church of Rome, by the time of Luther, had a list of seven principal sacraments: baptism, confirmation, the Mass, penance (performing spiritually improving acts of devotion or self-denial) anointing those who were seriously ill, ordination to the priesthood, and marriage. All were 'means of grace', and all were, of course, controlled and dispensed by the Church.

Protestants, in general, reduced the list to just the two 'biblical sacraments' – baptism and Mass/Eucharist/Holy Communion – and rejected all the other associated practices to do with relics and other holy objects. This was partly due to an aversion to popular superstitious ideas of religion as a form of 'magic', with the priest as the 'chief magician' muttering 'spells' in Latin. Some Protestants, of course, did away with sacraments altogether, notably Quakers and, more recently, the Salvation Army.

The Church

Here we do have something quite distinctive that arose from the thinking of the early Reformers. The medieval Church considered itself to be the 'Ark of Salvation', floating, like Noah's ark, as a God-given place of safety above the doomed world of sinful and lost humanity. There was no salvation outside the Church. There were, of course, two 'arks' at the time of the Reformation – the Church of Rome and the Eastern 'Orthodox' Church. But, for Luther and his contemporaries, it was the former that mattered. In stepping out of the ark, where did they find themselves? The answer, of course, was that they founded a new Church or, rather, a lot of new Churches. The more enlightened contemporary ecumenical view would be that there is only one universal (or 'catholic') Church, which includes

Rome, Orthodoxy, Protestants and all the rest. This is what the historic Creeds actually say – 'We believe in one holy, catholic and apostolic Church . . .'. But, of course, that is not what they originally *meant*: the 'One True Church' was the Church that published the Creed. And it was this that the Reformers called into question.

Indeed, the Reformers had, by and large, a very dismal view of the Church they had left behind, for they were denying, in leaving, that it was *the* Church. This was made somewhat easier, of course, if you identified the Pope as the 'Antichrist' of the Book of Revelation and, even more colourfully, the Church of Rome as the 'Whore of Babylon', or whatever. The problem was, in part, that medieval Europe had identified itself as 'Christendom', and everyone within Christendom was, *de facto*, Christian and therefore part of the Church. The Church and the State were, to all intents and purposes, one and the same. This view simply could not work for the Reformers, who, instead, looking to St Paul, identified the Church as 'the Body of Christ' (rather than the dominant Roman view of the 'Bride of Christ', drawn from St John, although St Paul does use this image). If the Church is the Body of Christ, each individual believer is a member of that Body. This leads to the concept of the gathered Church, the Church as believing community, distinct from the State and civil society. Where the Protestant Church became 'established' as the adopted state religion this distinction was somewhat blurred –hence, in England, the more radical moves towards separatism and independency.

The idea of the Church as, in some way, a distinct and gathered believing community is, most Protestants would agree, an important rediscovery of a New Testament principle. To belong to a Protestant Church you need to 'opt in' – you cannot really be *born* a Protestant. To suggest that you can would be to contradict several central Protestant beliefs, although in Northern Ireland, for example, 'Protestant' often has far more to do with ethnic origins and family political affiliations than it does with Reformation theological principles (apart, of course, from hatred of all things Roman Catholic).

The 'Priesthood of All Believers'

This equally Protestant emphasis follows on from what we have been discussing in this chapter. If the Church is a gathered community of believers, if faith puts all believers in the same position of dependence on divine grace; if the Bible is equally accessible to all who read it; if God is equally 'knowable' to all believers; if Holy Communion is not a priestly sacrifice; and if 'ordination' is not a sacrament – then what are we doing with 'priests'? The only 'priests' of the New Testament were the Jewish priests of the Jerusalem Temple. Christ himself is the one true, great 'High Priest' who makes the link between a holy God and sinful humanity. Other than that, the language of 'priesthood' applies to *all* believers together and equally: 'You are a chosen race, a royal priesthood, a holy nation, God's own people . . .' (1 Peter 2:9 – Luther liked this bit!).

Pastors, Ministers and Vicars

The New Testament does talk about certain specific tasks within the Church, and of particular 'offices' (like 'pastor' and 'teacher'), and it also uses words like 'deacon' ('servant' or 'minister'); 'elder' ('presbyter') and 'bishop' (*episkopos* or 'overseer'). Different strands of the Protestant tradition have selected different titles from the New Testament (such as 'minister', 'elder/presbyter' or 'pastor') to describe their office-holders and functionaries, while some (notably Anglicanism) have retained the traditional 'three-fold ministry' of bishops, priests and deacons. (Some Anglicans would argue that 'priest' is derived from 'presbyter'.)

In the Anglican tradition the term 'vicar' is often used for a clergyman (or, now, woman) – the term originally referred to someone who was a stand-in or deputy for a more senior clergyman. (The terms 'clergy' and 'clerical' themselves derive from an old word for 'clerk' – a reflection of the time when church personnel functioned as civil administrators.)

Such office-holders may, or may not, have formal titles like 'Reverend' and they may, or may not, wear distinctive clothes (the familiar 'clerical collar' and special robes or vestments). One distinctive echo, though, of Calvin's Geneva is the long black gown (sometimes worn with white 'preaching bands' at the neck) still often worn by Protestant ministers of many different denominations.

Some Protestant traditions have dispensed with identifiable ministers altogether, notably

Quakers and Brethren (see later). Others have retained a distinct 'hierarchy' of ministerial orders. Common to all, though, is the conviction that the Church is essentially the people, lay and ordained, who belong by choice, and sometimes the distinction between 'lay' (from the Greek word *laos* – 'people') and 'ordained' is rather more blurred than it is in the Roman Catholic and Orthodox Churches. So in a Baptist church, for example, anyone, lay or ordained, could be invited to 'preside' over the Communion meal.

It has to be said, however, that there is sometimes some ambivalence about the 'status' of ministers (or whatever they may be called) in many Protestant denominations: they may, in theory, be 'one of us', but in practice they are often 'one of them'! Overall, however, it would be true of Protestantism to say that the Church is identified with the 'whole people of God', all of whom are expected to play some significant part in its life and worship.

Predestination and 'the Elect'

No discussion of what Protestants believe would be complete without some mention of the doctrine, or teaching, most commonly associated with John Calvin. He believed and taught many other things too, most of them entirely uncontroversial and orthodox (with a small 'o'). But his views in this one area have become, to his followers, the test of 'sound doctrine'.

I'm afraid we have to thank St Paul once again! There is a passage in his letter to the Romans (in chapter 8) where Paul writes of those whom God 'predestined' to be saved. And out of this came the idea that only some, and not all, are ear-marked for heaven (remember our brief discussion on 'General' and 'Particular' Baptists in the early seventeenth century?). Those who are chosen will hear and respond to the 'call' of God – the rest will reject it, because they will be unable to do anything else: they were not chosen. They, unfortunately, are predestined, not for heaven, but for hell.

Sorry, but God is sovereign and you cannot argue with his will. How do you know if you are 'chosen'? You will have responded to the call of God, and be part of the Church. So, by definition, those who are 'in' are the chosen ones, and those who are 'out' have only a limited opportunity to come 'in' – it all depends on God's will. And if you do not respond to the call, you clearly were not chosen in the first place.

Now, whether all this is what St Paul actually had in mind, who can tell? (The passage probably has more to with Paul's thoughts about first-century Jews and Gentiles than it had to do with sixteenth-century Swiss burghers.) The good thing about this idea is that it should encourage a very strong sense of social responsibility and moral purity amongst those who consider themselves to be 'the chosen' or 'the elect'. They are, after all, hugely privileged. The bad thing is that those who believe themselves to be 'elect' might conceivably develop a spiritual superiority complex, even though they would be at pains to point out that they have been chosen in accordance with the divine will, and not on their own merit.

Like much Reformed thought, the idea of predestination was not original, but drew heavily on earlier thinkers like St Augustine and other 'Fathers' of the Church. This is a point worth stressing, because the Reformation was, in origin, a rejection of a particular aspect of the Church, at a particular time and in a particular place. It did not intend, at first, to reject all the previous 1,500 years of Christian tradition – despite the claims of some of its later followers.

And now, after this little bit of light relief, we must return to some more history.

Chapter 6

Revival & Expansion:
18th & 19th Centuries

Priests and Methodists

There were those who believed, after the first hundred years or so of Protestantism, that its mainstream and established forms were just too dry and dull, too wordy and rigid. Martin Luther's rediscovery of the power of divine grace and the assurance that this was sufficient for his forgiveness and acceptance by God seemed to have got lost somewhere. A certain 'Calvinistic clinical coldness' had, in much of Protestantism, overwhelmed this central 'conversion' experience. There was a desire, therefore, for something 'warmer', something more spontaneous and 'real', more inwardly convincing than just the intellectual rigour of Protestant theology.

This longing gave rise to what became known as Pietism. Pietism stressed a spirituality based on personal devotion and religious experience. It influenced both Lutheranism and Calvinism and became especially strong amongst the Moravian Brethren, under the influence of Count Nikolaus Von Zinzendorf (1700–60). It was the warm piety of the Moravians that was to impress a young Anglican clergyman who had trained for the priesthood at Oxford University – John Wesley (1703–91).

⊙ *General William Booth, founder of the Salvation Army, and a young Salvationist*

With his brother Charles and a friend, George Whitefield, they had earlier, in 1729 at Oxford, organized an earnest group of students (the 'Holy Club') to meet for Bible study and devotions, and to attend every church service they could get to – a zeal which earned them the nickname Methodists. But after a somewhat fruitless missionary journey to the United States in 1735 (and a failed romance) John Wesley returned to London where he encountered a group of the Moravian Brethren, having first come across the Moravians in America. And it was shortly after, at one of their meetings in 1738, that Wesley heard a reading from the preface to Luther's *Commentary on Romans* (there it goes again!). In a famous phrase Wesley was to say, 'I felt my heart strangely warmed'. This 'conversion' experience provided what had been lacking in his organized, but somewhat unrewarding, religious life – just the same effect as his brother Charles had experienced three days earlier.

The methodical Wesleys were great organizers and prodigiously energetic. John embarked on an exhausting programme of public preaching, frequently in the open air, and often with vast crowds gathering for the free entertainment. This regularly attracted considerable opposition from the Anglican establishment, and sometimes put his life at risk. British Methodists are still very fond of saying, 'Wesley preached here' and in the Methodist heartlands, such as Cornwall in the far south-west of England, there are numerous memorials, plaques and even 'Wesley Rocks' upon which he once stood to preach. His warm-hearted, simple and passionate preaching (40,000 sermons in all) had a tremendous impact, especially upon poor working people who often felt that they were overlooked by the wealthy and respectable Established Church.

The result of this was that the rapidly growing new movement – initially still within the evangelical wing of the Church of England – became more and more alienated from the Establishment. This was certainly not Wesley's intention, because he believed in revival from within. But it eventually led to the development of Methodism as a separate denomination, with its own ordained ministry. This was precipitated when Wesley, in 1784, appointed

Thomas Coke as, in effect, a bishop with authority to establish Methodism and ordain ministers in the United States.

Charles, meanwhile, proved to be a prolific hymn-writer, producing a remarkable total of 7,270 – not all as memorable as *Love divine, all loves excelling* or *Hark the herald angels sing*, but all written to help their often illiterate singers to memorize and understand the 'evangelical essentials' of Christian belief. George Whitefield (1714–70) travelled and preached widely too, and to great effect, not least in North America, where his visit inspired the Calvinist theologian Jonathan Edwards (1703–58).

Edwards' preaching, in turn, contributed to the Great Awakening of the mid-eighteenth century, an American revival which mirrored the impact of Wesley's preaching in England. This gave a great boost to American Protestantism, especially the newly arrived Methodism and the Baptist churches of the earlier settlers. North America produced its own Revivalist and Pietist hymns too, many of which found their way in to the later, and famous, nineteenth-century Sankey and Moody hymnbook (entitled *1,200 Sacred Songs and Solos*), still much loved by older evangelical Protestants.

The Nineteenth Century in England

That, of course, was not the end of it. No one knowing anything of the inevitable tendency of Protestantism to divide and multiply could imagine that the process would stop here.

Methodism, for all its initial evangelical fervour and heart-warming impact, developed over the next one hundred years into a denomination with many of the attendant qualities of the Anglican Church from which it had departed. Not surprisingly, some of its members became frustrated and disaffected, longing for something more authentic and 'biblical' than Methodism had been seen to become.

So Methodism spawned dozens of 'sub-sects', often in direct competition with each other, as can be seen in Cornwall, for example, where even a small village may once have had two or three different rival brands of Methodist chapel, ranging from 'Bible Christian' and 'Primitive Methodist' to 'Countess of Huntingdon's Connexion'.

In England there was also a growing concern that the Methodist Church was moving away from the more basic spiritual and social needs of the poor working classes, as Methodism tended to move into the middle class of society. The 'Protestant work ethic', coupled with the desire for self-improvement and education (frequently combined with teetotalism) had certainly fostered what we might today call 'aspirational values', as some of the splendid and once-prosperous nineteenth-century Methodist chapels clearly demonstrate.

This growing gap led William Booth (1829–1912), a Methodist minister, to start the Salvation Army in the poorest districts of Victorian London. It began as the East London Christian

Mission in 1865, becoming the familiar Salvation
Army in 1878. Like Wesley before him, he had
not intended to found a new denomination
but, inevitably, he did. And the Salvation Army
has earned an enviable reputation for its social
and relief work, often being the only Church

⊙ *A Salvation Army band from Penzance, Cornwall, photographed in the
1880s. General Booth is in the back row, wearing a top hat*

(although it has traditionally resisted that description) with any real 'street credibility'. In Britain it is still not unusual to see uniformed Salvationists witnessing publicly in town centres and public houses, where they usually get a respectful welcome.

One further movement from the earlier part of the nineteenth century that is still with us today is the Plymouth Brethren, usually known simply as 'the Brethren' and often to be found in 'Gospel Halls'. Although they trace their roots to Ireland, the first Brethren congregation was formed in 1831, in Plymouth, a major naval port in south-west England. The Brethren were distinctive in their rejection of all forms of ordained ministry, and in the simple and spontaneous nature of their worship – as in a Quaker meeting, any member of the congregation might speak as the Spirit led. And, like the Baptists, they practise 'Believer's Baptism' by total immersion. The Brethren have always been profound students of the Bible, with a particular interest in New Testament teaching about 'the end of the world'. As with the Quakers, the Brethren have often had an influence beyond their relatively small numbers.

Revivalism and Pentecostalism

Meanwhile, in America . . . While Methodism grew to become a large and prosperous denomination, there were those who (as in England) still longed for the heart-warming piety and personal religious experience that had brought it into being. This took a number of forms, typified by the Holiness churches. Racial and political tensions, especially focused on the issue of slavery, and resulting in the Civil War of 1861–65, further divided the mainstream Churches and sparked off the formation of new ones, especially amongst the Black American population. More vibrant and emotional forms of worship gained popularity as expressions of the revival of 'old time religion'.

One particular phenomenon began to appear in Holiness churches as well as elsewhere – glossolalia or speaking in tongues. St Paul listed in his letters a number of 'spiritual gifts' (Greek *charismata*) including one described as 'speaking in tongues'. This may have its origins in the story in the Acts of the Apostles, where the disciples, inspired by the Holy Spirit, spoke of 'the mighty deeds of God' in other languages, for the benefit of the cosmopolitan Jewish crowd who had gathered in Jerusalem for the Feast of Pentecost. In Paul's first letter to the church at Corinth he seems to be describing some kind of nonrational 'ecstatic utterance' rather than rational speech in a known foreign language and, subsequently, 'speaking in tongues' of this nature has been an occasional and noted feature of religious revivals down the centuries. The 'gift of tongues' at nineteenth-century American (and English) Revivalist meetings was of the 'ecstatic utterance' variety, and its effect was considerable. This is where the charismatic movement has its roots, as do the Pentecostal churches, which can be traced back to the earliest years of the twentieth century.

'Holiness' and 'Pentecostal' churches formed all kinds of loose affiliations and interconnecting networks, and soon spread back to Britain, where they gained some popularity. The charismatic movement is one that has touched every denomination, both Protestant and Catholic, in the last few decades. In some instances it has had a great uniting effect; sadly, in others, it has been more divisive. The same can be said of the 'evangelical movement', of which more later.

These various nineteenth-century spin-offs from the earlier Protestant traditions (and we could add many others, such as the Churches of Christ, the Seventh Day Adventists and the Christadelphians) still, broadly, belong to that historic 'family' of Churches. But there are a number of other religious movements that began in nineteenth-century America which moved in directions that make it difficult to identify them as 'Protestant'. Many have become very significant, ranging from the fringes of Christian orthodoxy to somewhere else altogether! They include, amongst many others, Jehovah's Witnesses, Christian Scientists and Mormons. Their beliefs may not be Protestant, but they are, nonetheless, distant cousins on the family tree. The proliferation of cults in twentieth-century America, some harmlessly wacky, others rather more sinister (more Waco than wacky), provides yet more evidence of what happens when you let people think for themselves (or rather, as too often happens, when they let other people think for them). Had he known where religious freedom would lead, would Martin Luther have torn down his theses before anyone had time to read them?

Chapter 7

Church Buildings & Worship

We shall pause for breath before we embark on the final leg of our tour through the Protestant tradition, and examine a very practical question: what are Protestant church buildings like, and what happens inside them? That, of course, would take a very long time to answer, given that no two Protestant churches are quite the same. So in what follows we shall, inevitably, be making some generalizations. What I shall describe would be true, for example, of the buildings and worship in many Baptist, Methodist, United Reformed and 'low church' Anglican congregations in England (and not too different from their counterparts in Europe, South Africa, America and Australia). I am also describing contemporary practice – if you want to know what worship was like in sixteenth-century Geneva when John Calvin was preaching, the short answer was: 'long'.

Buildings and Furnishings – Pews and Pulpit

Allowing that Church of England worship *may* be in a one thousand year old former monastic abbey church, we must treat that as the exception.

⊘ *Holy Trinity Church, Folkestone, Kent, founded 1868*

Although, having said that, some of the older Protestant traditions have built some pretty splendid monuments to their days of influence and prosperity, especially in nineteenth-century England. And there are some great Lutheran cathedrals in Europe.

A 'typical' Protestant Nonconformist church building will tend towards the plain and solid, with an absence of towers, steeples and elaborate architectural fancy. In older buildings pews (generally very uncomfortable) will still be in

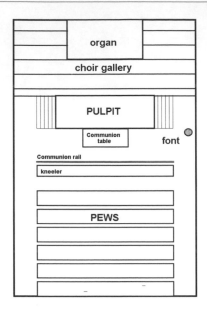

organ

choir gallery

PULPIT

Communion table

font

Communion rail

kneeler

PEWS

⊙ *Layout of a typical Nonconformist chapel*

evidence, possibly with numbers (and umbrella racks) attached. The numbers go back to the days when wealthier families paid 'pew rent' to get good seats near the pulpit, and there were 'free seats' at the back. Hence the sign is still sometimes seen stating generously, 'All seats are free'. Sadly, it is more likely now to be a case of 'Most seats are empty'. You may also find a small hole in the pew or seat-back in front of you. This is not alarming evidence of extra-large woodworm at work, but a sign that you are in a church where Communion is served in the seats in individual Communion glasses (see page 91).

When you enter, the first thing that may draw your attention is the pulpit. Whereas in a traditional Roman Catholic or Anglican church the altar is generally the focus of the building, a traditional Protestant chapel was built primarily for preaching, with a prominent, high, central pulpit overlooking the congregation. This reflects the Protestant emphasis on the Bible – the congregation quite literally 'sits under the Word of God'. In some Victorian Nonconformist buildings the pulpit reached quite dizzying heights, elevating the preacher high above his (very rarely her) hearers. In addition to the pulpit there will probably be a lectern to hold the Bible for the readings. It is likely that an open Bible will be prominent at all times when the building is accessible.

Organs and Guitars

Most traditional Protestant buildings also give a prominent place to an organ, reflecting the place given to hymn-singing within the tradition. This began with the hymns of Martin Luther (some, such as 'A great stronghold our God is still', are still sung today) and the unaccompanied singing of Psalms in sixteenth-century Geneva. Protestant hymnody really took off in the eighteenth and nineteenth centuries, notably with the Methodist revival. The late twentieth century has seen a vast production of contemporary-style hymns and songs, as well as (sometimes rather repetitive) 'choruses'. This is reflected increasingly in the use of other types of musical instrument (the 'trendy vicar' with his guitar has been augmented with drums and keyboards!) – the organ sometimes being reserved for weddings and funerals. The visitor should not be surprised to find evidence of hymns modern as well as ancient, with the overhead projector screen as much in evidence as a hymnbook.

Tables and Altars

Unless you are in a Salvation Army 'Citadel' or a Quaker Meeting House (both of which tend anyway towards a more austere simplicity) you will probably notice a table for Communion. This may be an elaborately carved stone altar in an Anglican church, or a plain wooden table in a Baptist church or Brethren gospel hall, or something in between. In many Protestant churches this will be empty of candles and crosses, with only a vase of flowers (flower arranging being, of course, the third sacrament in many churches!) when the table is not prepared for Communion. And in many Protestant churches this is more likely than not to be the case, because Communion can be an infrequent occurrence, unlike in Roman Catholic, Orthodox and Anglican churches, where it may be a daily event.

Monthly, quarterly or even less frequent Communion is not unusual in some Protestant traditions, although there has been a move in recent years towards more frequent celebration. Where the table is prepared for Communion it will probably, in many Protestant churches, consist only of bread on a plate and wine in a cup (or individual thimble-sized glasses – a peculiar Ñonconformist tradition driven by concerns about hygiene). And do not assume that the 'wine' is really wine – in many churches with a tradition of teetotalism it will be unfermented grape juice, or even blackcurrant cordial.

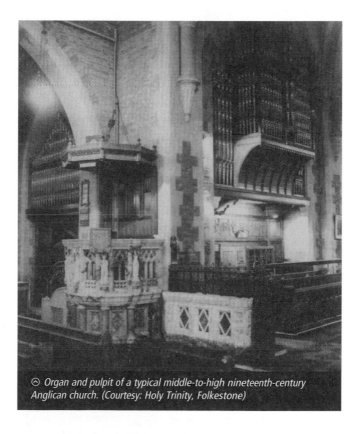

⊙ *Organ and pulpit of a typical middle-to-high nineteenth-century Anglican church. (Courtesy: Holy Trinity, Folkestone)*

Fonts and Baptistries

You can always recognize a Baptist church (and often a Pentecostal church or Brethren gospel hall) by the presence of a large hole in the ground (sometimes filled with water). This is the baptistry – large enough for the total, and often vigorous, immersion of an adult believer (see page 66). If you are fortunate enough to witness a Believer's Baptism, do not sit in the front row . . .

In other Protestant churches you will probably find the more familiar font, unless it has been put away in a cupboard for safekeeping. This is the stone or metal basin used for infant baptism. Generally it is to be found near the altar or Communion table, as a sign that the two sacraments are closely related, although sometimes a lack of prominence may indicate that this particular sacrament does not occupy a very significant place in some parts of the Protestant tradition. In others, especially Anglican churches, it is accorded the same high status as in the Catholic and Orthodox traditions and may well be a large and elaborately decorated feature of the building.

Signs and Symbols

In much of the Protestant tradition the emphasis is on simplicity, with few obvious features of religious art or decoration. So in older buildings there may be a war memorial or 'Roll of Honour', or a plaque commemorating past ministers or prominent lay members. Verses of scripture may be displayed, but any Cross (and there will not necessarily be one on view) will be empty – Protestants tend not to like 'crucifixes' which portray the crucified Christ, preferring the empty Cross of the risen Lord. There will probably be few, if any, religious pictures, and no statues of saints (apart perhaps from a discreet bust of John Wesley – a common feature of Methodist churches). And definitely no statues of the Blessed Virgin Mary, unless you happen to be in a 'high' Anglican church.

The earliest Puritans would have no images of any sort, and many beautiful medieval churches suffered terrible vandalism in the name of religious purity. Windows, where coloured, are likely to be in geometric patterns unless, of course, they bear the images of generous Victorian benefactors. Candles will probably only make an appearance at Christmas, although they are growing in popularity, now they have become more dissociated from dangerously Roman Catholic rituals! All of this, of course, is a broad generalization and, naturally, excludes Anglican churches, which may well resemble the 'Catholic' churches they once were, and still are in many cases, to all intents and purposes.

There are some ancient signs or symbols that are common to churches of all Christian traditions, notably the Cross (with or without the crucified Jesus). The fish is another ancient Christian symbol that often finds its way into church decoration. This reflects its close association with many gospel stories, notably the familiar miracle of the loaves and fishes and the feeding of the five thousand. This links the fish with the Communion meal, and it was also a secret sign used by the earliest Christians as a means of identifying themselves to each other, just as it has become a popular bumper sticker today. The Greek word for fish, *ichthus*, can be spelt out as *Iesus CHristus THeou Uios Soter*, which means 'Jesus Christ, Son of God, Saviour' – a neat summary of Christian belief. Another Greek abbreviation is also quite common, often on pulpits: the *chi-rho* Cross, which looks like an 'X' with a large 'P' on top. These are the first two letters of the Greek spelling of 'Christ'. The first three letters of the Greek spelling of 'Jesus' give the abbreviation IHS, which is found in many churches. Latin is also the basis of the abbreviation INRI: the inscription that Pilate put on Jesus's Cross – 'Jesus of Nazareth, King of the Jews'.

Worship – The Minister

You have come in and sat down, and had a good look around. What is likely to happen next? Again, whatever I say here is bound to be a generalization, with as many exceptions as examples. But in a 'typical' Protestant church the minister, or whoever is taking the service, will enter at the start, perhaps accompanied by some of the senior lay members. If it is an ordained minister, he or she may be wearing special robes, or a black gown, perhaps with a clerical collar and the white 'preaching bands' that came into fashion at the Reformation. (In all but the most staunchly Reformed and evangelical traditions it is now almost as likely to be a woman as a man.) Or the minister may simply wear a suit, or jeans and a jumper. Such diversity can be found in almost all Protestant denominations today: there is as much variety within most denominations as there is between the different traditions.

The Order of Service

The service may follow a printed, set pattern, or it may have the appearance of something rather more spontaneous. The use of prescribed liturgies, or formal, prescribed patterns of worship and prayers is a feature of some of the older Protestant traditions, although Baptists, for example, will rarely use them, favouring 'extempore' unrehearsed and spontaneous prayer (although it is rarely as unrehearsed and spontaneous as it may seem at first).

Congregational singing is likely to occupy some of the time (generally the congregation stands to sing, and sits and kneels to pray, although there are wide cultural variations in these practices in Africa, Asia and South America). Although they are becoming less common (often now replaced by a 'music group'), a choir may help to lead the musical aspects of the service. Bible readings are almost invariably a feature, and these will be accompanied by varying degrees of formality. In Anglican services, for example, it is common to stand for the reading from one of the four gospels.

The sermon, traditionally, has been the central feature of Protestant worship. In the nineteenth century and before, a good (or bad!) sermon could well exceed an hour – an act of penance for a congregation sitting in hard, cramped pews. Today, in the more evangelical parts of the tradition, the sermon may still occupy a sizeable part of the whole service, which in England is likely to be between an hour and an hour-and-a-half, but it could be much longer. This is a matter of culture as much as of theology – Protestant services in Africa may run for three hours or more. The sermon itself, if the church is true to its Protestant tradition, will probably be based fairly closely on a passage of the Bible or on a biblical theme, with some attempt to apply it to the contemporary situation of the congregation. In more evangelical circles, the congregation will probably follow the preacher's points (frequently three of them – another good Protestant tradition) in their own Bibles. So, if most of the congregation take their own Bibles to church, be prepared for a good solid, and probably long, sermon. The congregation may even be encouraged to join in with a discussion within the sermon, a practice that is becoming more widespread in churches of all traditions as 'all age learning' becomes popular.

Up to now, depending on the tradition, lay members of the congregation (who may also wear special robes, particularly in Anglican churches) will probably have been taking an active part in various aspects of the service: leading prayers, reading the Bible, preaching, giving their 'testimony' (again, a feature of more evangelical churches, where people are encouraged to talk publicly about their experience of God), even preaching. In most Methodist churches, indeed, it is very likely that a lay 'local preacher' will lead the whole service. And, of course, lay people will collect the offering, an indispensable feature of worship in almost all churches and one that may be attended by more solemnity than the reading of the gospel! Where the worship is of a more charismatic nature, do not be surprised if spontaneous interruptions seem to occur as members of the congregation make unscripted (and sometimes noisy) contributions to the service. This is in total contrast to the long periods of reflective silence that characterize Quaker worship.

If Communion is part of the service, there will be common features shared with most of the Protestant tradition, and distinctive variations too. In general, whatever else is included or left out, there will certainly be a prayer of thanksgiving for all that God has given, and a request to God that the Holy Spirit will, in some sense (which depends on the particular theology of the Church) make the presence of Christ real through the sharing of the bread and wine. At its climax will be the traditional Words of Institution, taken from the gospel account of what Jesus said and did at the Last Supper, and the bread will be symbolically broken by the person presiding at the Communion. This will almost always be an ordained minister, unless you are in a Baptist church or Brethren meeting. The issue of 'lay presidency' is hotly debated in many churches.

In an Anglican church, of course, you may get what is virtually the full Roman rite, with bells, incense and much kneeling and making of the sign of the cross. But in most Protestant churches it tends to be a rather simpler affair, emphasizing as much the congregation's active participation in the 'Eucharistic meal' as the preparatory words and actions. This participation may involve kneeling at a rail to receive the bread and wine (the latter either in a shared cup or chalice, or in the individual Nonconformist 'mini-cups' described earlier). Alternatively, the congregation may remain seated and be served where they are – the Baptist and Brethren tradition. In other words, no two Protestant churches 'do' Communion in quite the same way, which is only to be expected. Even the bread will vary, either being the Anglican-style thin 'unleavened' (yeast-free) wafers, or a crusty roll, or tiny cubes of sliced white bread. And the wine, as previously mentioned, is just as likely to be non-alcoholic grape juice, the distant memory of a nineteenth century tradition.

As will be clear by now, we frequently have to speak of the various Protestant traditions in the plural, rather than in the neat singular of the title of this book. For in most respects there is no such thing as the Protestant tradition, for Protestantism is a big, and diverse, family and, as with all families, there is no guarantee that all members of that family will resemble each other, or even get on together. So, as with belief, so with practice, any statement that begins, 'This is what Protestants do . . .' is probably going to be wrong in some important detail. But at least, if you wake up in the middle of a church service (a recurring nightmare for all ministers!) you will probably just about be able to work out if it is a Protestant one – unless, that is, it is 'Church of England', when you may get a little confused. Which is why we now need a whole chapter devoted to that subject.

Chapter 8

The Curious Case of the Church of England

You can't tell the story of the Protestant tradition without looking at the curious case of the Church of England, and Anglicanism in general. As will be clear by now, from the number of times I have had to say, 'apart from the Church of England', the Anglicanism of the Church of England, and its daughter churches, is really a distinct category, alongside Roman Catholic, Orthodox and Protestant. It emerged from the reforming movement that swept through Europe in the sixteenth century, but it developed in quite a different way from the Lutheranism and Calvinism of mainland Europe. For primarily political reasons, the Church in England removed the first (i.e. Papal) bit of 'Roman Catholic', but retained a great deal of the second bit – the 'Catholic'.

The split from Rome begun by Henry VIII was, however, the opportunity for English churchmen and theologians to develop some of the reforming ideas of Luther and Calvin – in particular, a more accessible form of public worship in the vernacular (common English), with an English Prayer Book and, ultimately, an English Bible. But, whereas the early Reformers had stressed that scripture was the sole authority in matters of faith and practice,

Ⓒ Henry VIII,
Elizabeth I,
Oliver Cromwell

the Church of England, while rejecting the authority of the Church of Rome, substituted its own ecclesiastical (Church) authority with the monarch as its head. Also, as with Luther and Calvin, there was an acknowledgement of the definitive teaching of the early 'Fathers' of the Church and the historic creeds.

This threefold appeal to the authority of scripture, Church and tradition was, in fact, identical to that of the Church of Rome – simply delete 'Rome' and insert 'England'. So, in effect, the Church of England looked very much like a modestly 'protestantized' Catholic Church, which is precisely what it turned out to be – a Catholic Church, with bishops, priests and deacons, but under English ecclesiastical and political control.

⊙ *Oliver Cromwell - 'a Puritan Independent'*

The Bible in English

This, perhaps, helps to explain why the Church of England has traditionally been suspicious both of Roman Catholics and of Protestants! So, for example, William Tyndale's thoroughly Protestant attempt to translate the Bible into English during the reign of Henry VIII led to his exile and subsequent burning at the stake for heresy. Miles Coverdale was somewhat more successful with his translation, based largely on Tyndale's. He survived exile and eventually became Bishop of Exeter. His translation of the Psalms was eventually used for the Book of Common Prayer. His Great Bible was published in 1539, and was followed by various other English Bibles, notably the Geneva Bible of 1560, which, as its name suggests, had a strongly Calvinist flavour. But it was not until 1611 that an official State-approved English Bible was published, under the authority of James I. This, of course, was the Authorised, or King James Version, which has had such a profound influence on the English-speaking Church, and the English language, ever since. The Church of England was prepared to have the Bible in the vernacular, but only if it was able to keep it under its own strict control. And this strict control extended to all aspects of belief and practice.

Intolerance and Rebellion – Cromwell and the Commonwealth

Even after the Elizabethan settlement, and the establishment of the Anglican 'middle way', the Church under James I was hardly tolerant of the more fervent English Protestants, many of whom remained in exile in the early years of his reign. The first Baptists, who gathered in London during his reign, had a hard time, as did the Congregationalists or Independents. It was not surprising, in this climate, that religious feelings ran high and, on occasions, threatened the monarchy. Roman Catholics as well as enthusiastic Protestants were denied religious freedom, and it was Roman Catholic activists who were behind the Gunpowder Plot of 1605, which attempted to blow up King James and his Parliament. The subsequent burning to death of one of the plotters, Guy Fawkes, is cheerfully re-enacted every 5 November (a distinctly English tradition!).

Later in the century it was the turn of Protestants to rise up against the King. The anti-royalist leader in the Civil War of 1642–46 was Oliver Cromwell, a Puritan Independent. The King, Charles I, was defeated in 1646 and imprisoned, ultimately to be executed. Cromwell had a clear Protestant agenda, and the success of his Model Army effectively spread religious Dissent throughout the British Isles. He attempted, unsuccessfully, to unite the Baptists, Presbyterians and Independents (the latter two finally came together in 1972, as the United Reformed Church). But he did succeed, for a short time, in disestablishing the Church of England and reshaping it as a Puritan national Church.

Imposed Uniformity

The Restoration of Charles II in 1660 brought this short-lived Protestant revolution to an end, and Puritanism was largely swept away under the 1662 Act of Uniformity, which thus defined Baptists, Congregationalists and Presbyterians as Noncon-formists. Following the publication of the *Book of Common Prayer* in 1662, only authorized Church of England services were allowed after the Conventicle Act of 1664, and persecution of both dissenting

Protestants and Roman Catholics was a sad feature of life in England for another two hundred years. The Act of Toleration in 1689 did allow Dissenters limited religious freedom, but this did not extend to Roman Catholics. (Indeed, full civil and religious rights were only granted to Roman Catholics and nonconformists in the nineteenth century.) If the Church of England has sometimes been reluctant to describe itself as 'Protestant' we can understand why.

» A 'Broad Church'

The story of the 'C of E', and subsequently of Anglicanism, is a long and complex one, and inextricably caught up with the English political and social history of the last five centuries. But we have seen enough of that story to recognize its influence on what is often described as a very 'broad church' – with elements that may look Protestant to a Catholic and Catholic to a Protestant, and the inevitable tensions that result.

So the 'low church', or more Protestant, evangelical parts of the Church may look with some suspicion upon the 'high church', Anglo-Catholic tendencies, and vice versa. The former is identified with an emphasis on the Bible and personal conversion, the latter with a more liturgical and sacramental approach to worship (sometimes rather unkindly called 'bells and smells'!).

Between these two poles there is a large mediating middle ground, from which vantage point (which I experienced as a child in a 'middle-of-the-road' parish church) Roman Catholics may seem alarmingly exotic, and the Free Churches somewhat dull and colourless.

Oxford Movement and Anglo-Catholicism

The division between the two extremes within the Church of England ('C of E') became very apparent in the first half of the nineteenth century. Oxford University (from where came the Methodism of the eighteenth century) was home to a number of influential high church Anglicans, who comprised the Oxford Movement. Notable amongst them were John Keble (1792–1866) and John Henry Newman (1801–90). They, with others, were alarmed at what they saw as a serious decline in the religious life of the Church of England during the eighteenth century (a rather dismal period in its history, by all accounts, in contrast to the success of Methodism). As an antidote they promoted a renewed interest in liturgy, ritual and a highly sacramental view of priesthood.

For them the Church was a divine, not a human, institution and thus distinct from the secular state. Although initially not intending to add the word 'Roman' to their brand of Anglican Catholicism, there was a drift in that direction which led Newman, most famously, to convert to the Roman Catholic Church, where he subsequently became a Cardinal. The Oxford Movement, however, saw itself as loyally Anglican and firmly rooted in the *Book of Common Prayer* and the Church of England's Thirty Nine Articles of Religion. Their views were promoted in the publication of a series of religious pamphlets, or tracts, which gave the movement the alternative name Tractarian. The Anglo-Catholic position has subsequently become very firmly established within the Church of England.

Evangelicals and Social Reform

The Oxford Movement was one reaction to the perceived decline in the religious life of the Church of England, and the growing influence of the secular thought and modern science that were the marks of intellectual liberalism. Another, swinging to the other extreme of the C of E, was the evangelical movement. Those low church, evangelical Anglicans, who had not become Methodists but had remained within the Church of England, were keen to resist both liberalism and what they saw as the alarming high church drift towards a decidedly un-Protestant Anglo-Catholicism. There was something of an Anglican evangelical revival, which encouraged those who were not inclined to sacramental and liturgical worship and who preferred instead a simpler and plainer style, with greater emphasis on the Bible in preaching.

Faced with the continuing, and rising, popularity of the Nonconformist denominations, and also recognizing that the Church of England was often conspicuously absent in many of the new industrial towns, with their growing social and moral needs, both evangelical and high church Anglicans founded a large number of new parishes during the nineteenth century. This explains why there are so many Victorian churches of all traditions. Both wings of the C of E were active in social reform, notably the abolition of slavery and the improvement of working conditions and social provision for the poor. Evangelicals were heavily involved in the great overseas missionary expansion of the nineteenth century, the formation of the British and Foreign Bible Society, and in the Sunday School movement, which was intended to improve the lives of working-class children. The Church of England generally was in the forefront of Christian social activity in that period, although Nonconformists were also active, especially in promoting education and self-improvement amongst the working classes, helping in the process to create a new, respectable, middle class.

The Last Hundred Years

It is probably true that these nineteenth-century developments determined the shape of the Church of England for the next century. The last one hundred years have also seen a tendency for the C of E to seek greater control of its own internal affairs, in the appointment of bishops or in authorizing different forms of worship – matters over which Parliament still has some control. Whether it has become more Protestant in the process is open to question.

Being the *Established* Church of England gives it significant privileges in national life, not least through its senior bishops retaining seats in the House of Lords (where they have recently been joined by prominent Nonconformist, Jewish, Hindu and Muslim peers, alongside the traditional representatives of Roman Catholic aristocracy).

As the nation becomes less attached to traditional forms of Christian religion, the debate about the meaning of 'establishment' becomes more pressing. Other historic established Churches elsewhere in Europe are facing similar questions.

The Rise of Evangelicalism

The polarization of 'high' and 'low' – Catholic and Protestant/evangelical – has, if anything, increased in recent decades. Growing cross-denominational alliances of evangelical and charismatic Christian groups have given added impetus to the more Protestant aspects of the Church. In the last ten years, for example, the Alpha Course, an informal group-based introduction to evangelical Christian faith organized by a successful (and wealthy) London parish, has proved exceedingly popular with many other Protestant Churches. Large-scale Christian festivals have become more common, and evangelical Anglicans are prominent at such events. There is, alongside this growth, a rapidly developing evangelical and charismatic culture of worship and spirituality. The 'Evangelicals' are a major force within the Church of England at the start of the twenty-first century.

The View towards Rome

Inevitably, the other end of the spectrum is becoming more 'Roman' in its Catholicism. The recent, and very often bitter, debate about the ordination of women to the priesthood still continues some years after the Church of England authorized the practice, prompting some high church Anglicans to seek refuge in the Church of Rome. Others have found the Orthodox Church more congenial.

This debate has raised all sorts of important issues amongst Anglicans, and has created all sorts of unlikely alliances. For example, is the Church of England free to make the decision to ordain women to the priesthood without the agreement of the Roman Catholic and Orthodox Churches? By what authority has it done so? Where does this stand in relation to scripture and the first few centuries of Christian tradition? Some strict evangelicals have argued that, according to scripture, leadership is exclusively male and have found themselves in agreement with high church Anglo-Catholics who have arrived at the same conclusion by a very different route, arguing that the practice of the Church of Rome should be the deciding factor.

Such a debate raises very interesting questions about where the Church of England sees itself in relation to those Nonconformist churches which have been ordaining women to the ministry for the last hundred years. And what does it actually say about the meaning of 'priesthood'? For those within the Church of England, especially women, the debate has been very painful. (Of course, the early twenty-first century is witnessing the traumatic arguments – far from over – about the C of E's attitude to homosexuality.) For those outside, these controversies are fascinating to observe, and suggest that the curious case of the Church of England will not be solved for some time to come.

Chapter 9

Protestants in the 20th Century

The previous chapter's look at the Church of England brings us almost to the end of the story of the Protestant tradition or, at least, to the latest chapter. Rather than look at individual denominations it is, perhaps, more helpful to look at some of the trends and issues that are common to all aspects of the tradition. The word 'tradition' may seem somewhat inappropriate if we are going to look at something as varied, even contradictory, as contemporary Protestantism. But that, of course, is part of its tradition.

Two of the most significant aspects of twentieth century Protestantism have been ecumenism and evangelicalism, so we shall look at these first.

Ecumenism

Given the fragmenting tendency inherent to the tradition it may seem an impossible task to try to reverse the flow and undo the divisions, but Protestantism has begun to attempt just that, as part of a wider movement amongst the Christian churches. There is a growing emphasis on deepening mutual understanding through dialogue and then, where possible, working more closely

⊙ *Emblem of the Diocese of Canterbury, England*

together with a view to healing some, at least, of the historical hurts within 'the Body of Christ'.

In England the process began amongst Protestants in the nineteenth century. Some of the older nonconformist denominations, as well as newer ones like the Methodist Church, came together under the 'umbrella' of the Free Church movement. This was, at least, a start because it gave an opportunity for discussion and action in areas of common interest or concern. Education was one of these, not least because the Church of England had, up until the nineteenth century, a virtual monopoly in that area. The major missionary impetus of the nineteenth century was another

reason for working more closely together.
Theological differences rooted in the heated debates
of sixteenth- and seventeenth-century Western
Europe were hardly going to help the work of the
missionaries in darkest Africa or remotest China.

The Edinburgh World Missionary Conference of
1910 was the start of serious efforts to overcome
what were, in some instances, centuries-old
conflicts. The trauma of two world wars provided
further impetus to get Christians to talk, work, pray
and worship together, and in a spirit of post-war
optimism the World Council of Churches first met in
Amsterdam in 1948. It comprised most (but not all)
of the Protestant denominations and the principal
Orthodox Churches.

The Roman Catholic Church was not initially
involved, but has subsequently become, first as an
active observer and now a full member. How the
Church of Rome has changed in the last five hundred
years is, of course, the topic for another, large book.
It is enough to say that the Reformation sparked off
a 'counter-reformation' in Rome which led to a whole
series of changes, with the result that the Church of
Rome today bears very little resemblance at all to the
one to which Martin Luther took such exception.
And the Second Vatican Council (1962–65), often referred to as Vatican II, which was initiated by Pope
John XXIII, produced a mood of revolutionary change
and renewal of which Luther and Calvin could
never have dreamt.

Vernacular worship; an 'inclusive' liturgy that
involves the whole congregation, and not just the

priest; much greater lay participation in all aspects of the Church's life and a startling openness to the study of the Bible have all come about in just three decades. The rate of change varies, dependent to some extent on the Pope of the day, but the process continues (not to the liking of all Catholics, it has to be said). All of this, inevitably prompts some enormous questions like, 'So what does it mean now to call yourself a "Protestant"?' And that question is all part of the current ecumenical agenda.

Ecumenism has been one of the significant features of the last half of the twentieth century, and it has seen some notable advances. Before this era, in 1925, Canada's Methodists, Congregationalists and Presbyterians formed the United Church of Canada. In 1972 the English United Reformed Church was formed by a union of Presbyterians and Congregationalists. And something very similar happened in Australia in 1977 to form the Uniting Church, and in the United States the United Church of Christ was formed in 1961.

Anglicans have had productive talks with Lutherans, reflecting their significant common ground in terms of eucharistic theology and practice, but this same issue, along with the meaning of ordination, has held up conversations between the Church of England and the Methodist Church. At the time of writing the negotiations continue. Similar conversations have gone on in New Zealand and the United States. The ordination of women, a common practice in most

Nonconformist churches, as well as now in the Church of England, is regarded by some Anglicans as a major stumbling block to further unity. It is a problem in any dialogue with the Roman Catholic and Orthodox Churches, but it is an essential part of the package in any moves towards closer unity with the mainstream Protestant Free Churches. This is an issue which may prove hard to resolve.

One notable, and early, development was the formation, with the Anglican Churches of India, Burma and Sri Lanka as full partners, of the Church of South India. This was inaugurated in 1947, with the active participation of the Methodist, Presbyterian, Congregationalist and Dutch Reformed Churches. The Church of England, part of the old colonial establishment, has viewed this development with some anxiety, it has to be said!

Overall the picture at the start of the twenty-first century is very different from one hundred years before. Some might say, cynically, that all of this is being prompted by anxiety over declining numbers of members in the mainstream Protestant Churches. While there may be some truth in this within the British Isles, where total numbers attending church are certainly in decline at the turn of the century, it cannot be true elsewhere in the world, where many Churches are seeing unprecedented growth. Perhaps, rather, it is the case that, while we cannot put the clock back and undo several centuries of history, we can at least try to wind the clock up and get it going again.

Evangelicalism and Fundamentalism

Another phenomenon of the twentieth century, and connected (both positively and negatively) with ecumenism, is the rise of evangelicalism. This is a confusing and often misunderstood term, so a brief explanation is required. Strictly speaking, evangelical means 'related to the *evangel* or gospel'. This is the Christian message of both judgement (of human sinfulness) and of promise (of forgiveness and new life). Both are consequences of the coming of God's kingdom of which Jesus Christ was the personal representative. It was summed up in his life and teaching, recorded in the four 'gospels' and proclaimed by the early Church.

The message of the *evangel* is 'repent, believe and follow', and its focus, of course, is Jesus himself. In that sense most Christians are, by definition, 'evangelical'. But the word has come to have a narrower definition (as in evangelism and evangelistic) which refers to the active proclamation of the gospel (also more narrowly defined) with a view to winning converts.

Thus some evangelicals have wanted to define both the content of Christian belief, and the nature of the conversion experience they associate with it, in more precise theological terms. Their belief is specifically in the idea (drawn, it will not surprise you to learn, from St Paul, although some would once again say that he has been seriously misrepresented in the process) that Christ's crucifixion was an atoning sacrifice, through which

God substituted his son's death for our own. This had the effect of absorbing God's righteous punishment for sin, so that we might be spared. Only, and precisely, belief in this idea can result in the one who thus believes being 'born again'. This reading of St Paul gained popularity at the time of the Reformation, and has defined, for many evangelicals, 'the gospel'. If you believe it, you are 'in'; if you do not, you are 'out'!

It is this narrow (and possibly mistaken) view of 'the gospel' that has led both to the success of evangelicalism and to further fragmentation of many Churches. Its success lies in the appeal to absolute certainty for those who are looking for simple answers to complex problems. It is part and parcel of an approach that claims 'the Bible says' with absolute conviction – and those who disagree are, by definition, in error. And this, as the twentieth century has shown, is powerful stuff. It leaves little or no room, of course, for those who may want to read the Bible in different ways, or offer alternative interpretations, or hold contrary views. And here is an inherent contradiction, since the freedom of both the congregation and the individual to read and interpret the Bible for themselves is *also* part of the wider Protestant tradition. There *is* thus the inevitable possibility of some real conflict. And this is precisely what has happened from Luther, and especially Calvin, onwards.

Conservative evangelicals (as they are properly called, in contrast to the more open-minded liberal evangelicals) were vigorously opposed to the emerging 'liberal' critical biblical scholarship of the nineteenth century, which was asking awkward questions about the origins, content and nature of the biblical texts, thus calling into doubt traditional views of the divine inspiration of scripture. There was also growing concern about the pernicious influence of modern science, especially Darwin's evolutionary biology, and anxiety provoked by the rise of the labour movement and socialism. There was, in particular, the threat of atheistic Marxism. All this led some conservative evangelicals to take action. In the face of creeping 'modernism' they insisted on a rigidly traditional view of the Bible and its divine inspiration, along with an equally rigid view of what constituted 'sound doctrine' and moral behaviour. Echoes here of John Calvin's Geneva, of course.

In 1895 a Biblical Conference of Conservative Protestants issued a list of five Fundamentals: the verbal inerrancy of Scripture (it was in every detail the precise record of God's actual utterance); the absolute and perfect eternal divinity of Jesus Christ; the virgin birth (or, rather, the 'virgin conception'); a substitutionary theory of the atonement (which we have discussed previously); the literal, physical resurrection and ascension, and the future bodily return of Christ at the Second Coming. All this was supplemented with a detailed explanation of how this related to the divine plan of history. Subsequently, in 1910, *The Fundamentals* were published and, at great expense, sent to three million American Protestant clergy, missionaries and students. This was sponsored by two wealthy American oil magnates. Within a few years Fundamentalism had taken hold in many Churches.

The most famous (or infamous) consequence of this was the 1925 Scopes trial, where a Tennessee teacher, John Scopes, was accused of violating a new state law prohibiting the teaching of evolution as scientific fact. He was fined $100. The case caused an uproar, yet, despite widespread concern about the implications of this verdict, Fundamentalism gained significant ground in both America and Britain. American Churches were split on the issue, and Fundamentalist groupings, such as the Southern Baptists, became exceedingly wealthy and influential. The appeal is obvious – absolute certainty of being 'saved', and knowing exactly what 'the Bible says' about everything, and being able to blame all evil (such as abortion or homosexuality) on Satan and his agents (who include all 'liberals' and socialists).

Fundamentalism, indeed, is often linked with extreme right-wing views as well as with detailed speculation about 'the end of the world' and 'Armageddon' – hence the very real anxieties about Fundamentalist cults at the recent turn of the millennium.

Fundamentalism is not peculiar to Protestant Christianity. It is also found in Judaism and Islam, for example. But it was extreme Protestantism that first coined the name. The historic links between Christian Fundamentalism and conservative American politics and business interests has, of course, been seen in recent years with the rise of the American far-right and the Moral Majority. (It is interesting to note, though, that the 2000 American Presidential election campaign moved away somewhat from this territory, even as British politicians have begun trying to woo the conservative religious vote.)

More spectacularly, the last fifty years have seen the rise of large-scale evangelistic 'crusades' which have moved into the TV and satellite age to great effect, as eloquent and flamboyant televangelists have (quite literally) sold their brand of Fundamentalist conviction to large and eager audiences. Sadly, the rise to fame of some of these has been matched by their subsequent fall into disgrace following embarrassing financial and sexual revelations. But all of this has given a very colourful tinge to the extremes of American (and, to a lesser extent) British Protestantism.

These excesses have, understandably, caused many evangelical Protestants to be more careful with the terminology they use. All Fundamentalists are evangelical, but quite obviously (although not always to the popular media) not all evangelicals are Fundamentalist. In a similar way, not all evangelicals are charismatic (discussed in Chapter 6), and vice versa. It is nowadays as important to grasp these terms as it is to understand the differences between, say, Methodists and Baptists because these categories divide within denominations as much as they unite across traditional denominational boundaries. And the media are apt to muddle them up when reporting, for example, the supposed excesses of an evangelist or the oddities of the latest charismatic phenomenon. (The much-publicised Toronto Blessing of the early 1990s is one example.)

Evangelicalism, as distinct from Fundamentalism, is now an accepted and respectable part of much of mainstream Protestantism, even if it has little resemblance to the earlier evangelicalism of Luther and Calvin. Billy Graham in America and the singer Cliff Richard in Britain both represent the 'popular' face of the evangelical movement, as do a growing number of media personalities and even the Archbishop of Canterbury in office at the start of the third millennium. Evangelicalism, indeed, is probably now the dominant 'flavour' of most Protestant denominations.

Leading Twentieth-Century Protestants

Having just mentioned one or two significant figures within the Protestant tradition we had better add a few more. Two of them are black, which is indicative of the shift in the ethnic balance of the Christian church over the last one hundred years. Two were theologians, and two might well count as martyrs. But none of them is a woman, which says something about the tradition – Protestantism has yet to produce its own Mother Teresa figure.

The first, from the early part of the twentieth century, is Albert Schweitzer (1875–1965). He was a

German theologian and missionary, as well as a prominent physician and musician. Schweitzer's ground-breaking work on Jesus and Paul was a turning point in theological understanding and helped set the agenda for twentieth-century biblical studies. He was one of those people who combine brilliance and passion in whatever they do, and he is widely regarded, and far beyond the Church, as one of the greatest world figures of the twentieth century.

Germany was where the Protestant Reformation began, and Switzerland is where its first major theological development occurred. And both countries have continued to produce influential Protestants. Karl Barth (1889-1968) was a Swiss Reformed pastor and professor. His *Commentary on Romans* (1919) – no surprises there! – brought him to prominence, followed by his monumental work on *Church Dogmatics* which urged a return to Reformation theological principles in response to what he saw as the dry and sterile approach to the Bible that had emerged in nineteenth-century German universities and influenced British and American thinking too. For Barth, God had revealed himself only in Jesus Christ and so any theology based on human experience or reason was futile. The Word of God, heard through faithful and obedient listening to scripture, is the only way to know God and his will for us. Barth's biblical theology has inspired some and appalled others – either way, he is regarded by many as the greatest theologian of his age.

Karl Barth found himself caught up in 1930s Germany, and eventually had to leave following his refusal to sign an oath of allegiance to Hitler. Which brings us neatly to our third prominent Protestant – Dietrich Bonhoeffer (1906–45). His age and his dates are highly significant because his staunch opposition to Hitler led to his death just before the end of the Second World War, at a tragically young age. He may have become one of the great post-war European thinkers, but instead was a martyr for his unshakeable Christian convictions. Bonhoeffer was a Lutheran pastor but, disgusted by the silence of the Lutheran Church in the face of the rise of Hitler, he joined the Confessing Church, which was founded in 1933 in opposition to the acquiescent 'German Christians' favoured by the Nazis.

Despite the obvious risks he insisted on returning to Germany after a period as a Lutheran chaplain in London. He became the influential head of a Confessing Church training seminary and wrote and spoke in ways that led to him being forbidden to teach and banned from Berlin. During the war he felt he had no choice but to actively oppose the evil that he saw in Nazi Germany and he became involved in a failed plot to assassinate Hitler. This led to his arrest in 1943 and, in 1945, just weeks before the end of the war, to his hanging. His writings, though brief, have proved to be enormously influential, not least in the area of the Christian response to the aggressive nationalism that was such a sad feature of twentieth-century Europe.

Bonhoeffer was not the only leading Protestant to die for his beliefs in the twentieth century.

Martin Luther King (1929–68) was a black Baptist minister in Alabama in the southern United States. Although slavery had been ended a century earlier, old white attitudes to the black population had survived and Black Civil Rights were a major issue in which King, as a Christian, felt he must be actively involved. Blacks were not allowed to sit on white buses and, in 1956 he organized a successful boycott of the bus service in Montgomery. From 1960 onwards he became a full-time civil rights activist, organizing nonviolent demonstrations and capturing the world's imagination with his eloquent 'I have a dream' sermon. In 1964 he was awarded the Nobel Peace Prize, and in 1968 he was shot dead by a white extremist.

Our final representative Protestant is still alive, though ill at the time of writing. Archbishop Desmond Tutu is the 'larger than life' Archbishop of Cape Town in South Africa. After Nelson Mandela he is probably the best-known figure in the story of the overthrow of the white minority apartheid government. He has been a powerful advocate of peaceful protest and now of reconciliation in South Africa, and has given the Anglican Church there a very significant role. The very different role of the ultra-Calvinist Dutch Reformed Church has also been an important part of that story, in providing the theological justification for apartheid – a further tragic illustration of how Protestants can all too easily find themselves on opposite sides of an argument.

Chapter 10

The Future of Protestantism

The world of the twenty-first century is a very different one from the Europe of the late middle ages. That is obvious, but significant. It raises some very important questions for those who stand somewhere within what we have tried to describe as 'the Protestant tradition'. Some of these questions are, of course, common to all members of the wider Christian family. As the Christian Church has celebrated the two-thousandth (give or take a year or two) birthday of its founder does it still have any meaning for today? Can we effectively translate ideas and images from the first century into the context and concepts of the twenty-first?

In an age where the traditional 'proofs' of the existence of God no longer make much sense to many people, are we to accept the twentieth-century's verdict that 'God is dead'? Traditional Christian views of the nature of the universe and its origins are still tenaciously held by a vocal few, but rejected by the great majority in the 'developed' world. Does that mean that the Bible has been proved wrong? Christian moral and social values do not seem to have had as much lasting impact on humanity as we may have hoped – is the world really a 'better place' than it was a hundred or two

⊙ *Traditional processional cross*

hundred years ago? As with so many other questions in this book, the answers are probably, 'Well, yes and no!'

But many would also want to say that the disturbing actions and compelling words of the 'carpenter from Nazareth' still jump out from the pages of the gospels that were written about him nearly two thousand years ago, and that the impact of his life and teaching can still transform the way we live and think today. And many would also want to say that the claim that 'he died and rose again' affects fundamental assumptions about ourselves and the universe in which we live, and about the God who created it. The Christian message still has the potential to turn lives, and societies, upside-down.

Christianity may still have something important to say, but what about Protestantism? After all, the 'big issues' faced by Protestants are faced by all Christians in all churches. The two modern Western philosophies of secular materialism and 'new age idealism' each pose a challenge to Christian, and not just Protestant, thinking, as do all the other contemporary 'isms' which (following the lead of Protestantism!) multiply so rapidly. The march of free-market capitalism and the subsequent global economy is welcomed by the wealthy, but is proving disastrous to the poor.

Advances in technology, especially when prefixed with 'bio-' or 'information', raise urgent questions about what it means to be human beings and about the nature of the communities in which we live. Questions of gender and sexuality, race and ethnicity demand our urgent attention, as does the relationship between all the world's religions, Eastern and Western. There is, I would suggest, a very pressing Christian agenda for the twenty-first century. But the question remains: is there still a worthwhile 'Protestant' agenda?

Most Reformation battles were long ago won (or lost), old enemies have changed sides, new alliances have been formed. The Church of Rome today bears little, if any resemblance to the one against which Martin Luther rebelled. 'Christendom' as a European sociopolitical and economic reality has not existed for a very long time. The map looks quite different and the ground out of which Protestantism grew is no longer there. Of course there are many things in our world still crying out for protest. But the sale of indulgences is no longer one of them. So it is sad that those who still, on occasions, vociferously identify themselves as 'Protestant' almost invariably use the polemic of the Reformers to do so.

We live in an age where, increasingly, to be a Christian means consciously 'opting in' to the community of faith, and that is becoming true of all Christian traditions in those Western cultures that may be loosely described as 'post-Christian'. And if the Bible is still a closed book to many Christians that is because they have not bothered to open it, not that their church still keeps it locked up.

Styles of Christian public worship and private devotion are drawing more and more on ancient, and shared, traditions, rather than on the conflicts of recent centuries, as a glance at the latest service books of, say, English Methodists, Anglicans, United Reformed Church, Catholics (and even Baptists!) quickly reveals. There is a growing shared 'repertoire' of hymns and songs that are shared by Protestants and Catholics alike. And you are likely now, in many Protestant churches, to find worship inspired by the contemporary Roman Catholic Taizé tradition, with candles in abundance, or to find aspects of Orthodox worship in use, even with icons in evidence.

And in Britain there is a growing interest in the early Celtic Christianity that predates even the Roman Catholic and Orthodox Churches, let alone the Reformation. Ancient holy sites are becoming places for Protestant, as well as ecumenical pilgrimage. The spiritual wells from which, increasingly, many people draw go much deeper than the last five hundred years. And most (if not all) welcome this turning tide.

In the light of all this there is a sense in which 'the Protestant tradition' can be seen as something that belongs more to the past than to the present, even though it still has its vocal and vigorous defenders. But many would feel that the old distinctions that marked out 'Protestants' from their fellow Christians seem, perhaps, rather insignificant in the twenty-first century.

Yet the connection between Church and State, between the 'spiritual' and the 'secular', is still important, as is the basis of authority – in the Church and in society. And what is the relationship between individuals and the communities to which they belong? How responsible are we as individuals for the way we choose to live our lives? Does freedom of conscience, choice and thought, and of open critical enquiry, still matter? The Biblical narrative still has a significant hold on human imagination: how should we read and interpret it?

Historically, these have been fundamental issues for Protestants, and have formed the basis for (sometimes radical) 'protest'. And this, I think, brings us to the real problem facing Protestantism. Many of the issues that brought it into being really are not significant any more. But some still are. The problem is deciding which matter, and which do not. And what if we find that the concerns which are still significant are ones that Protestants now share with most other Christians of most other traditions? What if the original Protestant 'protest' has served its purpose?

So, five hundred years on from Martin Luther, what should we be nailing to our church doors today?

Glossary

Anabaptist 're-baptizers' - a sixteenth-century movement which practised the baptism of adult believers, thus re-baptizing people who had been baptized as infants

Anglican part of the worldwide family of Churches (the 'Anglican Communion') directly related to the Church of England, with the Archbishop of Canterbury as the senior bishop

Archbishop the most senior office in the Anglican Church

Baptism (literally 'immersion') a form of religious 'washing' in water, to symbolize cleansing and acceptance by God

Baptists a movement that spread to England at the start of the seventeenth century, practising 'believer's baptism' and congregational Church government

Bible the sacred scriptures of the Christian Church, consisting of the Hebrew Bible (the Old Testament) and the earliest Christian writings (the New Testament)

Bishop a senior priest, usually responsible for a large number of churches and clergy in a geographical area called a 'diocese', and with the authority to confirm and to ordain priests

Brethren an evangelical movement that baptizes adult believers and which has no ordained ministers or priests

Calvinist relating to the teaching of John Calvin (sometimes also called 'Reformed')

Chapel a (small) church building, used for prayer and worship

Charismatic an emphasis on the supernatural 'gifts of the Holy Spirit', typically in spontaneous activity during religious services

Christening a common name for infant baptism

Communion the ritual sharing of bread and wine in a service, as a reminder of the Last Supper Jesus shared with his disciples, and as a sign of his death

Confirmation a sign of full church membership, involving (usually) a bishop laying hands on the heads of those being confirmed, blessing them in response to their public affirmation of Christian faith

Congregational a tradition that emphasizes government by the lay members of the local church

Conversion a conscious decision to become a Christian in response to the message of the gospel – a feature of evangelical churches in particular

Creed a historic statement of Christian belief, especially concerned with affirming the unique status of Jesus Christ

Deacon (literally 'servant') the lowest 'grade' of ordained ministry in Anglican and some other Churches; a lay office-holder in Baptist churches

Dissent the rejection of, and separation from, the Church of England by early seventeenth-century groups such as Baptists and Congregationalists

Doctrine the traditional and accepted teaching of the Church

Ecumenical an emphasis on the need for different Church traditions to overcome past divisions and work more closely together

Episcopalian a Church which has bishops (Greek *episkopoi*)

Established a Church, such as the Church of England, that is legally and constitutionally linked to the State

Eucharist another name for (Holy) Communion – commonly used in Anglican churches

Evangelical based on the gospel message of 'repent and believe', with an emphasis on conversion and personal faith

Faith personal belief in Jesus Christ and a commitment to follow his teaching and example

Free Churches Churches that, unlike the Church of England, are not 'Established'

Fundamentalism a belief in the literal truth of every word of the Bible, often combined with extreme political and social conservatism

God the supreme divine being, understood in terms of the Trinity of Father, Son and Holy Spirit

Grace God's free gift of love and forgiveness, received through faith in Jesus Christ

Holy Communion see Communion

Holy Spirit the 'third person of the Trinity' often described as 'God in action in the world', and particularly emphasized by charismatics and Pentecostalists

Jesus Christ the Son of God, who became a human being and died on the Cross, and who was then raised from the dead

Justification the classic Protestant doctrine of God's acceptance and forgiveness of those who have faith in Jesus Christ

King James Bible (also called the 'Authorised Version') the traditional Bible translation of English Protestantism

Lay/laity all the people of God, but usually taken to refer to the non-ordained members of the Church

Lord's Supper another name for Holy Communion, often used by evangelicals

Lutheran based on the teaching of Martin Luther

Methodism the movement founded by John Wesley as an evangelical alternative to the Church of England

Minister a common Protestant term for an ordained person

Nonconformism a later name for Dissent, in reaction to the 1662 Act of Uniformity, and still used to describe churches that are separated from the Church of England

Ordination the appointment, recognition and authorization of a priest or minister, usually at a special service involving the laying on of hands

Parish a geographical area, centred on a church, which is under the pastoral care of a vicar in the Anglican church

Pastor a local church leader, either lay or ordained, with a particular emphasis on the care of the congregation

Pentecostalism a late nineteenth/early twentieth-century charismatic movement

Prayer Book (the *Book of Common Prayer*) the official collection of services, prayers and regulations for the Church of England

Predestination a classic Calvinist doctrine which teaches that God has pre-chosen some people for salvation, and others for damnation

Presbyter (literally 'elder') an ordained minister in some Protestant Churches

Priest an ordained person (traditionally male, but now also female) in the Anglican tradition (sometimes regarded as a variation of 'presbyter')

Puritan a group in the early years of the Church of England which emphasized strict morality and purity in all aspects of religion and daily life

Quaker (Religious Society of Friends) the movement founded by George Fox, which emphasizes the inner nature of religious experience

Reformation the religious and political reform movement started by Martin Luther in sixteenth-century Germany which led to a formal separation from the Church of Rome

Reformed related in particular to the teaching of John Calvin

Salvation Army the social work and evangelistic movement founded by William Booth in nineteenth-century London

Separatism the belief that the Church should be entirely distinct from the State

Synod an important meeting for Church government, with responsibility for a large geographical area

Trinity the traditional Christian understanding of 'God in three Persons': Father, Son and Holy Spirit

Unitarianism the rejection of the doctrine of the Trinity, affirming that God is One, not Three

United Reformed a Church formed by the union of the Congregational and Presbyterian Churches

Vicar a priest in the Church of England, responsible for a parish

Appendix: Useful Addresses

Protestant Churches in the UK

These addresses (where available) are for some of the mainstream Protestant churches in the UK. Most of their 'head offices' will send you free leaflets and details of useful publications on request. For a lot more information, and for addresses elsewhere in the world, the best starting point is the World Wide Web.

Baptist Union of Great Britain
Baptist House, PO Box 44, 129 Broadway, Didcot, Oxfordshire, England OX111 8RT
www.bapfist.org.uk

Brethren
There is no national organization for Brethren assemblies. Some useful websites are:
www.crosswinds.net/~cbav/cbwho.html
www.storm.ca/~sabigail/faqs/brethren.htm
www.geocities.com/Athens/2394/assemblies.html

Church of England
The Enquiry Centre, Church House, Great Smith Street, London, England SWIP 3NZ
www.church-of-england.org

Church of Scotland
Church of Scotland, 121 George Street, Edinburgh, Scotland EH2 4YN
www.churchofscotland.org.uk

Church in Wales
Church in Wales Centre, Woodland Place, Penarth, Wales CF64 2EX
www.churchinwoles.org.uk

Methodist Church
Methodist Church House,
25 Marylebone Road, London, England NW1 5JR
www. methodist.org
Religious Society of Friends (Quakers)
Friends House, 173–177 Euston Road, London, England
NW1 2BJ *www.quaker.org*
Salvation Army
The Salvation Army, 101 Newington Causeway, London,
England, SE1 6BN *www.salvationarmy.org.uk*
United Reformed Church
Life & Witness, United Reformed Church House,
86 Tavistock Place, London, England WC1H 9RT
www.urc.org.uk

Other UK Church Organizations
Council of Churches for Britain and Ireland
(main ecumenical body)
www.ctbi.org.uk
Evangelical Alliance
(main 'umbrella' group for evangelical Churches in UK)
186 Kennington Park Road, London, England SE1 1 4BT
www.eauk.org.uk
Protestant Truth Society
(a good place to look for very 'traditional'
Protestant beliefs)
184 Fleet Street, London, England EC4A 2HJ
www.ptslondon.btinternet.co.uk
For useful information
www.churchnet.org.uk

Worldwide Organizations
World Council of Churches
(masses of useful information about all sorts of things)
www.wcc.coe.org/wcc/english.html/
National Council of Churches in Australia
www.ncca.org.au
Canadian Council   of Churches
www.web.nef/~ccchurch
Conference of   European Churches
www.cec.kek.org
National Council of Christian Churches in the USA
www.ncccusa.org
Worldwide Anglican Communion
www.anglicancommunion.org
For lots of facts and figures . . .
www.adherents.com

Index